SHADOW WORK
=[for Hot Messes]

Transform from **CHAOS** to **CLARITY**
by Embracing Your Authentic Self

Mandi Em
Author of *Feral Self-Care*

Adams Media
New York • London • Toronto • Sydney • New Delhi

Dedication
Dedicated to my inner demons, unexpected mentors in the school of consciousness, curiosity, and love.

 adamsmedia

Adams Media
An Imprint of Simon & Schuster, LLC
100 Technology Center Drive
Stoughton, Massachusetts 02072

First Adams Media trade paperback
edition October 2024

ADAMS MEDIA and colophon
are registered trademarks of
Simon & Schuster, LLC.

Simon & Schuster: Celebrating
100 Years of Publishing in 2024

For information about special
discounts for bulk purchases, please
contact Simon & Schuster Special
Sales at 1-866-506-1949 or
business@simonandschuster.com.

The Simon & Schuster Speakers
Bureau can bring authors to your
live event. For more information
or to book an event, contact the
Simon & Schuster Speakers
Bureau at 1-866-248-3049 or
visit our website at
www.simonspeakers.com.

Interior design by Julia Jacintho
Images © 123RF

Manufactured in the United States
of America

1 2024

Library of Congress Cataloging-in-
Publication Data has been applied
for.

ISBN 978-1-5072-2299-7
ISBN 978-1-5072-2303-1 (ebook)

Contents

Phase One
Perception: Seeing the Unseen...19

Phase Two
Investigation: Getting Cozy with Your Shadow...97

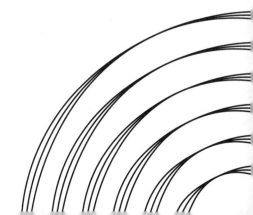

Phase Three
Integration and Synthesis:
Vibing with Your Whole Self...163

Introduction

Have you ever been in a situation where you've behaved or responded to something in such a way that made you think, *What the hell was that??*

Do you ever get the restless feeling that you aren't living up to your true potential and who you truly are?

Do you find yourself feeling like there's themes and repetitive patterns of bullshit popping up in your life like an insane case of universe whack-a-mole despite your best efforts to make it stop?

If you answered with a full-body "fuck yes!" to some or all of these questions then congratulations….You've encountered a very normal (albeit distressing) dimension of the human experience: your shadow. Simply put, your shadow is a part of your subconscious, aka all the mucky, repressed stuff that loves to hide deep in your mind and then pop out at you when you aren't expecting it. Luckily, *Shadow Work for Hot Messes* is the supportive guide and vibe-checking bestie you need for approaching, unearthing, and integrating your shadow. This workbook takes you through the kind of "boots-on-the-ground," trudging around in your own mess, healing WORK (with a capital EVERYTHING) that actually crafts a solid foundation for finding peace, authenticity, and confidence in yourself and your life. You'll go from a hot mess, to…well, still a hot mess, but one who embraces those messy parts as a piece of what makes up the wonderfully unique human that you are.

You'll start with a quick section on how to use this workbook, including the types of activities you'll be doing, and a self-contract for you to sign as a promise to yourself that you are committed to this work. Then, before jumping into the trenches, you'll learn more about the basics of shadow work itself, including the three important phases of identifying, exploring, and incorporating your shadow. This section will help you get all prepped and ready for more than fifty activities that lie ahead, such as exploring deeper questions through writing, sifting through the important events of your experience with a personalized life map, and having a candid conversation with your shadow.

If you have picked up this book, then get hyped: Forging a relationship with your shadow is not only possible, but can also be incredibly healing, illuminating, and dare I say...even fun?! To learn about your shadow and all the tricky, icky ways it may be tripping you up along the way doesn't have to be a mopey or guilt-fueled endeavor. On the contrary, it can be immensely liberating and exciting to not only get to know yourself better, but to uproot the tentacles of the monsters harbored within that are messing with your flow. Are you ready to face the hot mess?

How to Use This Workbook

This workbook is meant to be approached in an interactive way. Consider it the encouraging best friend whose sole mission is to help you spark the torch that illuminates your shadows, find your way home to yourself, uproot your bullshit and fears, and more! Feel free to talk to the pages, holler at them when they attack you, and put the whole damn book in a drawer when you're ready for mercy. Feel free to hug it when it helps you feel "seen," toss it in your bag for accessibility, and doodle in the margins so you don't lose track of any breakthroughs!

Shadow Work for Hot Messes will be talking to you as well, with creative prompts such as Write It Out, Fill It Out, and Sign It Out. Space is provided for you to do this work within the pages; however, if you want to do some of these over and over (which is highly encouraged as shadow work is *not* a one-and-done endeavor), or are using an ebook version, feel free to use a separate notebook or journal to complete the activities.

This book is organized into key parts: an introduction to the shadow, an investigation of the three phases of shadow work (perception, investigation, and integration), and a conclusion on how to move forward from this book in an empowered way.

Each of the three phases has been broken down further into chapters that cover the important parts of that phase. It is in each chapter that you will get to interact with the things you are learning by writing answers to more in-depth questions, and sometimes drawing, talking out loud, filling in blanks, and more. And while there is a distinct part on integration, there are also additional integration tips sprinkled through-out each chapter. These tips will provide supportive vibe checks, more exploratory questions, and suggestions for how to move forward following the chapter lessons and activities.

When first using this workbook, you'll want to go through it chrono-logically. Dealing with the shadow is a process, from the first glimmers of perception to the finishing touches of ongoing integration. Of course, on every subsequent pass through the workbook, you can jump around here, there, and everywhere based on the elements of your shadow and shadow work that need a little TLC at a given time. In fact, that shit is highly encouraged! But it's advised to go that route only after you've done a solid once-through.

Please understand that the examples used in this book are used for illumination purposes only. Some may ring true for you, while others may not. The shadow is a complex and nuanced topic that manifests differently for different people. Any examples used are simply to get those mind juices flowing, and not intended to trigger, attack, or sway you. If any discussions or perspectives within these pages trigger some big feelings, take advantage of that bonus opportunity to explore what nerve is being poked and why.

Ultimately, this is a workbook to help lead you back to *yourself*: aka the very best teacher and guide there is or could ever be for the wholly unique, brilliant mishmash of feelings and experiences that is your life.

Shadow Work Basics
So You Wanna Dive Into Your Shadow Side?

Although the concept of the shadow and the power of your inner darkness has been explored and emphasized in different cultures throughout human history, the shadow self as understood in modern times was popularized through the work of Swiss psychologist Carl Jung. In his models of the psyche, Jung explored the interplay between the conscious and the unconscious (the latter of which houses the shadow self).

The conscious mind is the shit *you know* you know—your own awareness of your personality, thoughts, feelings, who you are, etc. When people discuss the mind—the essence of an individual's, personal beliefs, motivations, etc.—this is the part they are referring to.

The unconscious mind, however, is where a whole host of other shit is happening, under the radar, yet influential as fuck regardless! This is where your shadowy demons hide—your repressed memories, emotions, and beliefs. It's a behind-the-scenes cast of chaos that can pop up in subtle and not so subtle ways throughout your life to mess with your flow.

Imagine you were trying to keep your house clean, but there was a secret staff that would come in when you weren't home, tracking mud on the floor and dumping out your drawers. This would make the task unnecessarily difficult and borderline impossible. Similarly, healing and personal development work that focuses only on the conscious aspects of your experience is a frustrating and often-sabotaged task. Once you recognize there is a shadowy team that may be sabotaging and interfering with your shit, you can view things with a little more perspective and begin to sort out how everyone can start moving forward on a united page.

The Collective Shadow versus the Personal Shadow

Just as we as individuals are not the whole story in the larger context of our communities, society, and world, we as individuals are not the sole holders of shadow. Jung's model of the psyche also includes the collective shadow in the collective unconscious.

The collective shadow bleeds into your worldview and life experience, and you can see it reflected in some of the worst parts of humanity. Xenophobia, war, terror—all of these tendencies not only lie within the most hidden corners of the individual psyche, but in the bleakest corners of the psyche of our species. To put it simply, the collective shadow is the repressed shadow side of humanity at large.

Now, because this workbook you're holding in your hot little hands only contains so much space, and the goal here is *personal* healing, you will be focusing on the personal shadow. However, it is important to note that the personal shadow is influenced and fed into by the collective unconscious, just as the rain that falls is drawn from the oceans and seas around the world. So this concept of the collective shadow, though not a main focus of the workbook, will be referenced at times throughout. If you're at all interested in more robust learning about the collective unconscious/shadow, I would strongly urge you to check out Jung's many works, or the many subsequent books by other authors inspired by his theories and approaches.

The Goal of Shadow Work

The overall goal of shadow work is self-knowledge and wholeness. In practical terms, this means a life that's less fueled by underlying fuckery and experienced more in positive ways. Once you're aware of your shadows and can treat yourself with love and compassion (even when you mess up), you'll be less likely to engage in self-sabotage, and more likely to break maladaptive patterns in your life and relationships. You'll be able to identify and work with the heavier and more complex feelings you may have, instead of running from or suppressing them.

Side effects of doing shadow work and integrating your unconscious demons into your conscious awareness may include:

- Increased confidence and self-esteem.
- Less living your life dictated by fear and shame.
- Increased ability to not lash out in present situations based on past experiences.
- The ability to form better relationships with less shitty people.
- The ability to recognize when others may be operating from their own shadows.
- More comfort in your authenticity.
- A sense of clarity regarding who you are, so you can live with intention and improve self-trust.
- Better life satisfaction.
- More openness and acceptance toward others.
- The ability to process triggers or challenging emotions more quickly.

And that's just a sampling of the awesome things that may result!

Your Shadowy Road Map: The Three Phases of Shadow Healing

When it comes to shadow work, there's a tendency for teachers and guides to throw a vague mystical mist atop it all, dropping cryptic buzzwords like "integration" and "shadow healing" with no practical explanation, leaving most of us to wonder what the fuck any of it even means. The two questions I hear again and again when it comes to shadow work are, "How do I begin?" and "How do I integrate the things I uncover about my shadow for lasting change?"

In efforts to speak directly to those two questions in particular, I teach shadow work as occurring in three phases:

1. **The Perception Phase:** Noticing that your life may be impacted, held back, or at the mercy of some shadowy bullshit.

2. **The Investigation Phase:** Finding where these shadows came from and took root.

3. **The Integration and Synthesis Phase:** Using the information you collect from Phases 1 and 2 to make lasting change in your life.

Each of these steps are not only distinctively important, but they are also important as part of the unified whole of the shadow work process. For example, a focus only on Phase 1 will lead you to the vague idea that there's some bullshit happening in your life, whereas a focus only on Phase 2 will give you no clear sense of what to do with the information you're discovering, much less why that information matters.

Like the unified psyche, all phases have their place and provide a complete process that can accomplish big things!

Write It Out

Now that you understand the phases of this process, is there any phase in particular where you feel "stuck"? For some, recognizing the shadows might come easy, but figuring out how to integrate them might be a challenge. For others, figuring out how to find the roots (the investigation phase) might be tricky.

Write out your initial thoughts/first impressions regarding these phases of shadow work:

_____

_____

_____

_____

_____

_____

_____

_____

_____

_____

_____

As you move through this workbook, keep in mind these initial thoughts. You might find that you are more plugged-in than you think, or you might find that a lot of this stuff feels brand-new. No matter what, getting a sense of where you're starting and where you're going will help you along the way.

Tools, Materials, and Spaces

Given the sensitive and vulnerable nature of shadow work, it's important to approach shadow work as you would the psychedelic experience. The right tone and environment for your active work (much like the concept of "creating sacred space") are key. It can be an emotionally jarring experience to face your shadow, so it is important that you feel safe and relaxed. Particularly when it comes to having shadows associated with trauma and pain, you should take the opportunity to ensure you aren't approaching it in a heavy-handed way, which could make it a negative experience (not very motivating!) and erode your self-trust. The following activities and prompts are intended to help you set the scene for your shadow work. It's best to set yourself up somewhere cozy and private that feels familiar and safe.

Set the Mood: A Shadow Work Playlist

Beyond the motivation of listening to a song that you like, it can be helpful to shadow work to create a playlist that calms your nervous system. After all, shadow work can be an emotional undertaking.

To get you started, write out some specific songs or genres of music here that help you feel calm, safe, and secure:

_____

_____

_____

_____

_____

_____

Write It Out: An Inventory of Tools and Vibe Checks That Make You Feel Safe

In addition to sound, different environmental prompts can signal safety or coziness for you, whether it be certain colors like blue or green, scents like vanilla or clean linen, textures like fuzzy blankets, etc.

Make an inventory of the things in a space that help you feel comfortable and secure:

_____

_____

_____

_____

_____

_____

Set It Up: A Personal Protection Ritual

A personal protection ritual can be a great way to bring the feeling of safety into your shadow work efforts. Essentially, you combine your calming playlist with cozy environmental prompts to make the experience of working with your shadows feel safe. For example, if you found that the scent of rose and the color green help you feel calm and safe you may want to create a ritual where you spray rose water around your space, and wear green or wrap yourself up in a warm green blanket, hygge-style.

Create your own personal protection ritual using your Inventory of Tools and Vibe Checks activity answers as inspiration:

_____

_____

_____

_____

_____

_____

_____

_____

_____

_____

_____

_____

A Final Note on Shadow Work

As you move through this book, take care to listen to your body and spirit. The purpose of all these healing efforts is to feel better, not worse. Shadows have a sneaky tendency to undermine healing work efforts, focusing more on guilt and shame rather than understanding and accepting. We must seek shadow illumination to find self-understanding, not just for the sake of feeling bad and fulfilling shadowy desires to linger in spaces where we feel like we're stuck. If the latter scenario sounds familiar, it's time to cut it out! If it isn't empowering or helping you heal, shut that shit down, recalibrate, and try again later.

Also, please recognize that some shadow work, certainly in cases of significant trauma, is best done under the guidance of a trained therapist or mental health professional. Know and honor yourself enough to give yourself the resources and support you need to best tackle this work.

Your Shadow Work Self-Contract

To start things off with a bang, take a moment to truly commit to the mission of this book: unveiling and integrating your shadow in an effort to bring more peace, clarity, and authenticity into your life! Are you willing to see this through as a gift for yourself? Can you make a promise to yourself *and* keep it? Can you commit to allowing yourself to be a priority like this?

Read and initial each statement, customizing as necessary, making a promise and commitment to yourself:

_____ I, _____, hereby commit to diving into the realm of shadow work in the spirit of love, acceptance, and self-compassion.

_____ I commit to facing my demons, repressed bits, and shadowy void space with the end goal of finding integration and wholeness that will bring practical, mental, and spiritual empowerment as I move forward in life.

_____ I additionally acknowledge that perfection is not the goal, and that shadow working is a process that all of us can tackle, even if I feel like a hot mess, and I love and accept myself.

_____ I make a commitment to myself that I will check in with my mind, body, and spirit to know when to push through to do the hard things, and when to take a break in the spirit of loving self-care.

_____ I commit to allowing fun and playfulness to be my allies along the way.

_____ I also commit to let this be a journey of healing and exploration and not just another place to feel shame, guilt, self-judgment, and other icky self-deprecating shit. I will do my best to vibe check those, and shift into the gears of unconditional love and acceptance.

_____
[Sign Here]

Phase One

PERCEPTION
Seeing the Unseen

The first of the three phases of shadow work is the perception phase. This, to put it simply, is just the part of the process when you begin to notice that there may be a shadow issue fucking with your peace. Think of this as the glimmer that causes you to notice that there is work to be done!

In some cases, folks are drawn to the shadow work arena piqued only by a vague curiosity or conscious decision to learn what it's all about. In other cases, the desire to delve into the shadowlands may have stemmed from a particular event, such as an episode of particularly cringy self-sabotage, or a tantrumy display, such as losing your shit on a friend or stranger. Episodes that may feel so out of alignment with who you *think* you are that they made you deeply question *what the hell is actually going on* inside to have elicited that response! All paths to this work are valid and must be approached in the spirit of compassion, grace, and curiosity.

The purpose of this phase of the work is simply to take inventory of the patterns, situations, and expressions of your shadows made manifest in your everyday life. This isn't to say that you will have a notable shadow issue every day; just begin making note of the mundane expressions of your shadow self and how they might be influencing your experience of this wild and beautiful life. Each chapter in this part has corresponding examples, integration tips, and prompts to help you deeply connect to the concepts within, including uncovering self-sabotage, and exploring your personal mythology and lore.

As stated earlier in this book (and will be again and again until the repetition vibrates through every cell in your very being!), this work is an exercise in compassion, exploration, and love. The inquiry you engage in to explore your shadow sides and find the deep roots within is an act of self-love. Tough love, perhaps; but love, no less.

So as you move through this phase, keep your heart and mind open, and keep the shadow work comfort strategies discussed earlier in this book close. It's some hot mess hand-holding for the quest to explore the shadow realms inside yourself!

Chapter 1

The Invisible Villain
Patterns When Your Shadow's Pulling the Strings

There are many baffling things we humans experience, but something that can be particularly unsettling is the sensation that we are not driving the ship. And I don't mean a lack of control in the realm of life itself, with its many complex and intertwining outside variables. I mean that feeling of *personal* helplessness, as if there is some malevolent force with its tentacles deep within us, playing us like a puppet.

It's easy to believe, based on the subjective experience of being alive, that your conscious awareness is what's pulling the strings of the meat machine you pilot. This is what forms your values, your actions, and the things you believe to be true. However, most of us also have a great deal of subjective experience with the *opposite*: We can find ourselves in situations and patterns (both interpersonal and intrapersonal) that can feel so dramatically outside the realm of anything we would logically want, that it can leave us wondering who is really running the show after all.

Much like the oft-cited metaphor of the iceberg, that which is in your conscious awareness is only *part* of the story, baby! There is a vast and rich ecosystem of both bloom and bullshit that dwells in the land of subconscious awareness—meaning, that which you may not be fully cognizant of. As already discussed, this is the realm of the shadow, and you can have many demons and unintegrated aspects of your awareness housed within.

It's more common than you might think to find yourself in repetitive patterns that can reflect just how much pull the shadow in your unconscious mind has. These are certain situations or themes you find playing out over and over again (despite your best efforts to avoid them)—like dating someone with the same issues you saw in your parent and swore you'd *never* put up with in a relationship, or running away from potentially amazing friendships at the first tiny hint of conflict.

Now, before getting much further: Since you might be reading this nodding and thinking, *OMG, this is exactly what is happening for me!*, it would be reckless of me not to put a pin in it here for a moment to give you a chance to get that shit out so you can move forward full throttle.

Write It Out

Stop and reflect for a moment: Are there any specific patterns that you feel tend to come up in your life over and over again? These can be patterns in interpersonal relationships, overarching themes, or situations and circumstances in your life. Write that shit out.

_____

_____

_____

_____

_____

_____

_____

_____

_____

_____

_____

_____

_____

_____

_____

_____

Now, if you didn't have a lightning-strike real-world connection to tie this to then don't worry! Later in this chapter you will have more space to sit with this question and reflect on the answer. Remember: There is no timeline on healing. Let yourself marinade on this if you need to!

The point is, despite our best efforts to create lives that feel supportive to us, many of us can find ourselves "trapped" in these patterns enacting the same situations and melodramas over and over again. To the point where it can feel downright spooky, or like we're getting screwed by fate.

These patterns can manifest in shockingly diverse ways, and can be pervasive and truly hard to shake. In my own work with others, I've seen people who have found themselves dating similar personalities over and over again (right down to small details of their partners' lives, including family structure, health, etc.), people who've had the same career dramas despite changing the particular field they work in, and more. Truly the possibilities are endless, and once you see the specific ways your own patterns have been cropping up in your life, you cannot *unsee* them!

Some general examples of how these patterns can manifest:

- Meeting the "same" triggering or oppressive personality over and over again manifested in different people (e.g., the emotionally distant partners you gravitate toward, or friends who always ask for your help but never offer to help *you*).

- Winding up in the same situation repeatedly despite making your best efforts to avoid it (e.g., the number of people who somehow always find themselves in dire financial straits, even if they've gotten a windfall of money or won the lottery).

- Finding yourself enacting the same patterns or roles in multiple relationships across the lifespan (e.g., forever the "bad guy" or the "victimized empath").

The list goes on and on!

Although making note of these patterns is a great first step, it is only *part* of the story. In many cases the invisible villain pulling the strings for these relationships and situations to occur is your shadow, and some work needs to be done in the realm of your subconscious worldview or belief systems in order to shift things. (You will dive into this further in Phase 2.)

Before I go on, I'd like to clarify that this isn't just some victim-blaming take on how you're attracting bad experiences into your life and all the bad shit you have or will ever encounter is a direct result of your fucky vibes or whatever. The truth is that being alive is fraught with chaos and variables that we have utterly no control over. There is truly no way to control or anticipate *all* of the things *all* of the time. Circumstance, opportunity, and pure dumb luck will always have a seat at the table in the grand high council of how your life goes.

However…

In many cases, your shadow is all up in the mix pulling strings like an unhinged puppeteer.

Think of it this way: Suppose you hold a shadowy belief that you are fundamentally unworthy of love, or that other people can't be trusted. You might find yourself subconsciously drawn toward relationships where you are treated in ways that confirm this belief. Or imagine you have this shadowy desire for power that's been repressed since a tumultuous childhood where you didn't have any feelings of security at all. You might find yourself in situations as an adult where you are constantly placed in roles where you feel responsible for controlling things. In both cases, you may not *like* or *consciously consent to* the patterns you find yourself in, but these patterns may be serving your shadows in some way.

Please believe me when I say that you are worthy and able to have more and better than what your shadows may have you believing. The future is full of unknowns, and the roads you have not yet traveled may not be accurately predicted or determined by fuckery in the past.

⚡ Integration Tip

Your shadows picked up an affinity for these patterns long before you were able to consciously consent to them. You can reclaim your power by reframing the patterns as contracts you have the power to break rather than fixed destiny or "curses" that you have no control over.

Write It Out

So take some more time to reflect on the patterns that may be popping up in your life, investigate the recurring themes, and try to get a sense of what you're working with so you can get a clearer picture of what to explore further and what needs shifting. Since you're at Phase 1, the perception phase, of this workbook, this is the time to simply practice nonjudgmental awareness of the fact that there may be themes and patterns that are playing out in your life story. Earlier in this chapter you were given a space to get out your initial thoughts, now is your chance to explore the patterns of your life more fully (feel free to revisit this topic if more things come up later).

Reflect further on these patterns:

_____

_____

_____

_____

_____

_____

_____

_____

_____

_____

_____

_____

_____

Chapter 2

The Scourge Behind the Curtain
Looking Out for Self-Sabotage

From the outside looking in, being a person seems pretty straightforward. If you want to *do something*, do it (or learn how). If you want to *change something*, figure out where you're starting and where you want to go. If you want to *be the best version* of your hot mess lil' self, just define what that looks like and take the proper steps.

Easy peasy, right?

Unfortunately, this kind of borderline delusional best-case scenario experience is the furthest thing from *easy peasy* for most people. Life in action is messy, clouded with feeling and drama, and when it comes to doing what's in our best interests, the truth is that most of us do... well...*not* that (not easily, at least).

Let's pause here for a moment. Before moving forward, answer the following prompts:

Write It Out

List five things that feed your soul and make you feel great (energized, fulfilled, happy, etc.):

1. _____   4. _____

2. _____   5. _____

3. _____

List five things that drain your energy or spirit, or just make you feel bad:

1. _____   4. _____

2. _____   5. _____

3. _____

Now go back and ask yourself how frequently you spend your time, energy, and attention on each of these ten things:

_____

_____

_____

_____

_____

_____

_____

_____

Despite the fact that operating in your own best interests to achieve your desired ends is simple enough in theory, it typically only appears that straightforward when viewing *other* people's lives (or, when viewing your own from a more enlightened place such as within the psychedelic experience or after mastering meditation—rare). Once actually *in the shit*, this human life is an immersive and emotional experience that doesn't often afford you the luxury of perceiving things in a way that's quite as simple as it appears on paper.

The bird's-eye view of many lives would show that people often say they want one thing, then do something else altogether. Or they decide to follow a certain linear path, but instead of getting from point A to point B, they tap dance and flail around in a bewildering display of aimless chaos! In many cases, self-sabotaging fuckery like this is a direct result of shadowy urges and influences at play. Much like an invisible villain that puppeteers bullshit without your conscious awareness or consent, aspects of the shadow can also act as the Coyote to your Road Runner: the sneaky saboteur!

If the concept of self-sabotage seems all too familiar, that's probably because it's unlikely there's a human on this planet who *hasn't* experienced it in one form or another. Self-sabotage is exactly what it sounds like: It is behavior (either *doing* things or *not doing* things) that isn't in alignment with your goals or the things you think you want. It's doing things that are not supportive of (or are in direct opposition to) your desires or what's best for you. It may also include unconsciously-yet-willfully messing up the things you already have or taking a metaphorical baseball bat to the progress you've already made.

It's a crazy, yet totally normal, expression of your humanness!

From the outside, self-sabotage can look like laziness, recklessness, or just plain foolishness. But the root of self-sabotage is far more complex. From a shadow work perspective, you must find it to be the hidden scourge behind the curtain, the sneaky bastard waiting in the wings for the perfect moment to set fire to your peace!

Write It Out

What does self-sabotage typically look like for you? Answer these questions to explore:

1. Read through this list of Common Flavors of Self-Sabotage and check all that feel familiar:

    ☐ Relationship instability (e.g., causing unnecessary conflict through insecurity, projecting, or expecting another person to be responsible for your happiness)

    ☐ Maintaining bad habits or neglecting self-care

    ☐ Letting important things slide (procrastinating)

    ☐ Being reactive rather than proactive

    ☐ Striving for perfection, or waiting for perfection before taking action

    ☐ Telling yourself you're shit

    ☐ Making excuses to not do difficult things

    ☐ Pushing yourself too hard or not listening to your body (which typically, in turn, makes you depleted or sick)

    ☐ Not having boundaries with yourself and your time

    ☐ Addictions and obsessions

2. In my life, self-sabotage has looked like (use the answers to the first question to guide you):

_____

_____

_____

_____

3. I am usually aware of when I am in a cycle of self-sabotage:

  ○ Yes   ○ No

4. Is it possible my self-sabotaging is ever fulfilling a need somehow, or keeping me feeling safe? (These questions may spark some uncomfortable aha moments for you; you will be diving deeper into the role of shadows as fulfilling needs and how to integrate those needs in Phases 2 and 3 of this book.)

  ○ Yes   ○ No

Add any additional thoughts about self-sabotage:

_____

_____

_____

_____

_____

_____

_____

_____

A difficult truth (that once understood is utterly life-changing) is that most people will only go as far as their opinion of themselves will take them. To put it metaphorically, you will never fly if you *believe yourself unable* to fly. You will never rise if you are holding yourself back. And you will not allow yourself to receive things you believe yourself unworthy of or incapable of having. Yes, the shadow can contain repressed negative traits such as anger, desires for power, and the tendency to manipulate, but it can also contain the positive light aspects of you such as your confidence, creativity, and unhinged authenticity! And if you feel as if you have no light, or that you don't *deserve* to be lighter, then you may find yourself perpetually wandering around in darkness.

Self-sabotage is one of the ways that your shadows manifest to dim your light. You may find that you set yourself up for failure as a form of self-sabotage because despite desperately *consciously* not wanting to fail, you believe that you will or that you aren't worthy of succeeding. Since this part of this workbook is all about perception, let's find the perceptions you have about yourself that fuel your urges to torpedo your own progress.

Write It Out

The following is a list of prompts. As you read them, all you have to do is write down what you feel in your body, and where you feel it. That's it! If you feel your guilt and shame shadows rising up with their "not enoughness," feel free to take a deep breath and urge them to fuck off entirely. Again, you cannot fight shadows with shadows; you cannot fight shame with more shame. The game is illumination, baby! This means shining the light so you can later take steps toward accepting any and all of what you find.

Read the following prompts, and write down what you feel in your body, and where you feel it:

I am able to set goals for myself, then take necessary steps to achieve them.

_____

_____

I trust that I am worthy of my desires.

_____

_____

I believe that it's possible for good things to come to me.

_____

_____

I trust myself to make good decisions with the info I have available to me.

_____

_____

I'm open to loving myself more in words and in actions.

_____

_____

I'm open to allowing good things to happen to me, and noticing when they do.

_____

_____

"Success" feels...

_____

_____

"Failure" feels...

_____

_____

⚡ Integration Tip

Although we often look at it in a negative light, most of the time "failure" is just a honing or learning process where we likely end up with more info than when we started. Yes, even self-sabotage is a lesson. It's like a crash course on personal development in real time. Alternately, what is success? If you don't have a solid, crystal clear idea of what this will look and feel like, then you will likely always feel as if you're falling short. In many cases, a lot of self-sabotage can be thwarted by reframing your ideas of success and failure, alongside powerful self-concept work.

Chapter 3

Mundane Maintenance
How Your Shadow Affects
Your Self-Care

By now you're probably getting a good sense of how the shadow tends to operate—like a vaudeville villain creeping about and twirling its mustache as your conscious awareness does its best to cope under the illusion that it's the one calling all the shots!

Let's talk for a moment about the way this creeping entity can affect one of the most powerful dimensions of mundane existence: your practical daily self-care. This is an often neglected and underappreciated aspect of existence, even though it's the "routine maintenance" element of making sure that you are keeping up and integrating any other personal development or self-love work! Without self-care, you can fall right back into the same traps of self-neglect, burnout, and feelings of being "stuck" that can have you working on yourself for ages with little to no lasting results.

Consistently abandoning your self-care is another form of that sneaky self-sabotage you explored in the previous chapter!

The importance of mundane maintenance in your personal growth plan can be illustrated like this: Imagine doing a lot of self-love or confidence work, then going back to a day-to-day dumpster fire routine where you treat yourself like shit. Or perhaps you decide to make improvements to your health or wellness routines, but still stay up until 3 a.m. watching true crime specials and covered in chip dust and the vague scent of self-loathing and regret—obviously not the best first steps to reaching your wellness goals!

This mundane maintenance kind of self-care is not only good for you; it also supports the shifts you're trying to make in your more obvious healing and growth efforts. It helps you ensure that you can *actually hold and maintain* any progress you make, so you're not just left spinning your wheels.

Now, "self-care" is a broad term that can cover a lot of ground, but for the purpose of this chapter, you are going to focus on the things that involve generally taking care of yourself (mind, body, and spirit). For example:

- Doing the things that make your body feel good, even if it requires putting off instant gratification, or doing things that may not necessarily hit the dopamine tap in the moment. In other words, all that annoying "taking care of your physical vessel" stuff, such as eating fresh healthy foods, exercising, and getting a good night's sleep.

- Doing the things that support your mental wellness, such as journaling or not doomscrolling yourself into needing a midday depression nap.

- Doing the things that make you feel lit up on a soul level, such as working on your art, spending time with friends, dancing, or just vibing.

Consistently neglecting your self-care is something that's incredibly easy to do in the modern-day hustle culture. In today's society, self-sacrifice can often seem virtuous—glorified even! The cold hard fact is that most are coasting in survival mode in this culture, despite all of our modern comforts (obviously your mileage may vary here). And from a shadow perspective, many people may neglect daily self-care not *only* because they have to fight to find the time and energy to put toward it, but also because deep down they may carry some fucky beliefs about whether they are even worthy or permitted to designate their own wellness as a top priority!

Write It Out

When it comes to your self-care in the realms of body, mind, and spirit, how well would you rate how you currently attend to yourself?

Write out some good things you are doing for each, as well as where you might be neglecting your care:

   1. Body

_____

_____

_____

_____

_____

_____

   2. Mind

_____

_____

_____

_____

_____

_____

3. Spirit

_____

_____

_____

_____

_____

_____

_____

The shadow can manifest in your mind, body, and spirit in a variety of ways. In the mind, you can beat yourself up over a past mistake, stick to unsupportive thought patterns about what you believe to be true and possible for you, and circle-jerk your demons to squeeze every last drop of negativity and self-confirming "badness" from them. Example: A person who knows that they feel better when they do their morning hype-bitch statements (aka affirmations) may fall off of doing them once they feel as if it's started to work because their shadowy belief that they do not deserve to feel more empowered and confident gets roused.

In the body, people most commonly self-sabotage personal care by neglecting physical wellness. This involves things like not getting enough sleep, feeding yourself harmful substances or otherwise _not_ nourishing yourself well, and engaging in risky behaviors that can cause physical issues. Example: A person who squashes their big shadowy feelings with junk food, drugs, or other physically harmful/depleting behaviors.

In terms of spirit self-care, your shadow may aid in self-sabotage by keeping you from doing the things you love or causing you to find fulfillment in all the wrong places (even if those places are draining for you in the long term). Example: A person putting their efforts of spiritual self-care into using a certain belief system to try to control others or force those beliefs on them.

Since every human is unique, with different goals and opportunities when it comes to self-care, it's worth taking the time to define what mundane self-care would look like for you. As with most things, having clear definitions and goals can help; you need to know what you're working with or striving for in the first place, so you'll feel motivated to see that vision through.

Write It Out

Answer the following questions to further explore what self-care means to you:

1. What does taking care of yourself mean to you?

_____

_____

_____

_____

_____

2. What would caring for your mind, body, and spirit look like and feel like in practice?

_____

_____

_____

_____

_____

Most people deeply know how important self-care is. When confronted with friends' or family members' struggles to prioritize it, many (without a second thought) will hype them up with an inspiring diatribe about how necessary it is for healthy survival. Yet once you see that same struggle coming from *inside the house*, the energy may change and you might begin to lean into a "not for me, though" vibe when it comes to your own personal care. It can be helpful to first recognize that this is happening, then use your heart and your logic to give yourself the same grace, support, and permission you'd give any other person in this situation.

As discussed in an earlier chapter, the beliefs you have about yourself on a subconscious level can be incredibly powerful for both the big and small things in your life. These beliefs form the foundation upon which a vibey, supportive life can be built. What are some of the beliefs and attitudes you have about self-care for yourself?

⌇ Integration Tip

In many cases, a failure to prioritize self-care is just a symptom of deeper wounds and shadows relating to worthiness and self-trust. To integrate the shadows that contribute to this kind of chronic self-neglect, you must recognize that you do not have to "earn" your wellness Give yourself the permission to prioritize your own care needs, or permission to start the confidence and self-love work that will help you unapologetically land at the top of your own priority list!

Chapter 4

Who Are You?
Exploring Your Personal Mythology and Lore

Although "who are you?" may seem like a simple question, it's pretty fucking loaded, and how we answer can reveal a lot about our self-concept, and how we think about the bigger story of our lives.

So, who are you?

Many would answer this question with things like name, age, job title, familial roles (mother, father, etc.). However, these are just some characteristics. Who are you really? Surely you can dig deeper than just the bare-minimum census data! Perhaps you'd describe yourself in terms that more broadly define your emotional qualities or experiences like Empath, Optimist, Pessimist, Survivor, Fucked-Up Human Having a Fucked-Up Human Experience….However, these are just descriptors as well—too brief to capture the essence of who you really are.

Who you believe yourself to be has a lot to do with the stories you tell yourself, and the characters and archetypes you resonate with. Everyone has a personal narrative of their existence. This includes who you are (identity), your life story (themes), and where you believe yourself to belong in the larger scheme of things. Some elements of this personal narrative are supportive (for example: "I'm a great friend to others"), and some are decidedly…*not* (for example: "I'm unlucky in love").

Ultimately, you are the active creator, main character, and also passive consumer of this body of stories, and you have bold and persuasive power over how the story is not only written and conceived, but also how it's subjectively perceived. However, most of this occurs on a subconscious level, which means you do not feel an active conscious awareness of it. Instead of steering the ship of their own story, many people get the overwhelming sense that they are the subject of some cosmic joke, or the passive target or plaything of the fates.

Can you recognize the power you have?

Write It Out

Answer the following questions to explore your main character energy:

1. As the main character of your life, how would you describe yourself?

_____

_____

_____

_____

_____

_____

_____

2. If you had to write a blurb or plot summary/synopsis of your life thus far, sort of like a movie trailer, how would it go?

_____

_____

_____

_____

_____

_____

_____

_____

Doing shadow work is intrinsically serious business; however, you can inject a little fun into the heavy bag of bullshit by approaching some of this work in the spirit of play. Life feels how it feels. Whether the victim, the hero, or the villain, you have already been feeling all that up 'til now. You are already immersed. A little perspective can allow you to see your life through the spirit of play and reconstruction. By filtering your stories through a veil of personal mythology and lore, you can get that space and perhaps find a little character development along the way.

Before going further, it would be helpful to have a clear understanding of myths versus lore:

- **Myths:** narratives used to interpret, understand, or communicate important values or information (these are usually sacred; for example, think of the mythology of ancient Greece and the purposes these stories held).
- **Lore:** the gathered collections of stories (narratives) about a certain group or thing (a good example would be the personal lore of your own family).

In academic contexts, myths are viewed as being a part of larger lore structures of specific groups. For the purposes of your own life, this shit is applied to the personal lens of subjective experience. For example, a personal myth could be that time you overcame adversity through coming out the other side of some significant, life-altering event. (Part of my own personal myth is overcoming a lot of mental health instability and trauma in my youth to find empowerment and peace as an adult.) And personal lore could be particular achievements (such as being able to play piano by ear) or experiences (such as that time you went traveling to South America to "find yourself") that have become a part of your narratives about yourself.

Your personal mythology and lore contributes to your self-concept. → Your self-concept determines your reality. → And your reality forms the foundation of the actions you do or do not take, or how you react to the shit in your life.

By conceptualizing your life and identity in this way, you can essentially start to "hack" your identity, gain perspective of the stories and roles you're living out, and craft your next chapters!

Write It Out

Describe some of the circumstances or occurrences that could be classified as having "myth-level" status in the story of your life:

_____

_____

_____

_____

_____

_____

Now write out some of the significant aspects of your personal lore:

_____

_____

_____

_____

_____

_____

⚡ Integration Tip

Can you look at your personal myths and lore and ask yourself whether these are supportive stories? Are you giving yourself main character status and allowing room for character development? If these personal narratives aren't supportive, consider looking at them through a different lens (much like those movies that look at the same events through different character perspectives).

Now you may be thinking, _What does this level of storytelling have to do with the shadow?_ Well, given the fact that your shadow contains repressed unintegrated bits of your awareness, sometimes your memories, and even your core wounds/fears, etc., it has a _lot_ to do with the shaping and perception of these tales.

For example, people can go through similar positive or negative experiences and yet walk away envisioning themselves as the hero or victim depending on how they frame these stories to themselves and how they feel toward themselves in general. For some, a chaotic and neglectful childhood can just be an obstacle way back in the rearview mirror, a dragon already slayed. For others, it can be an ever-present backseat driver as they try to navigate life through adulthood. That isn't to say these interpretations should be compared to one another, just that knowledge of how you interpret and envision this stuff can help you gain helpful perspective moving forward.

Write It Out

Connect your myth and lore examples with how these narratives may be contributing to your unique collection of shadows:

_____

_____

_____

_____

_____

_____

_____

_____

_____

_____

Whether or not you've consciously wrangled control of the lore of your own muddy, drama-fueled existence yet, it does indeed form the basis of your subconscious operating system. The lore includes memories, traditions, and accumulated wisdom. The lore of who you are—your transformations, triumphs, and tribulations—forms a rich backdrop for how you see yourself and connect with your families, your history and lived experience, and who you are becoming. It provides a framework for what you see as possible for your future, and a map for how you may position yourself in dynamics with other people. In other words, it's pretty powerful fucking stuff!

Chapter 5

What Kind of "Parent" Are You?
Caring for Your Inner Child

Something that's important to remember when approaching shadow healing is that the shadow is not just a dungeon for your hidden, repressed, "uglier" traits. Much like your outward self, the shadow can be a contradictory clusterfuck of light and dark, rad and bad! As discussed in the first part of this book, some good things can be hidden in there, bright and positive little pieces of you that have been dimmed and hidden, duct-taped and banished into the basement of your awareness!

In many cases, your wounded "inner child" might be seeking refuge in those hidden places.

Like the shadow, the concept of the inner child is typically associated with psychologist Carl Jung. The essence of it is this: We all carry remnants of the child we once were inside of us. The temperament and disposition of this inner child can vary significantly depending on the types and quality of experiences and messages you received while you *actually were* that child in real time. The whole spectrum of perspectives and feelings of what life was like for you as a child can be reflected in this inner stowaway. It can be a heightened sense of wonder, creativity, and joy; a foot-stomping, tantruming force to be reckoned with; or a small, frightened creature with an overall feeling of helplessness.

How would you characterize your inner child?

Draw It Out

Think about your inner child. On first impulse, what do they look like and how do they feel? What are your inner child's deepest needs and desires? What is their personality? Draw it out on the following page, and feel free to write any notes about what came to mind as you brainstormed how your inner child would look. And please note you do not have to be an artist for this, so feel free to go cartoony, abstract, or any other style that feels the most comfortable for you!

For adults with a healthy connection to their inner child, feelings of joy, play, and delightful curiosity may be accessible and easy to tap into. It may also be easier for those precious few to cope with and integrate tantrumy inner child urges with compassion and grace. The presence and voice of the inner child may bring delightfully curious and novel energies to their lives when it comes to problem-solving, managing emotions, and finding the fun in the day-to-day. For others, whose inner child may be carrying heavy bags of trauma and pain, the connection with this aspect of the self may have been severed as a coping mechanism to move forward.

The issue with being disconnected from your inner child is that children (inner or not) have a tendency to hijack your awareness and sabotage your peace by any means necessary when their needs for love and connection are unmet! When your inner child's needs aren't being met, you may find yourself feeling helpless, small, or unloved, and these feelings may cause some seemingly irrational or mischievous shadowy behavior.

It's important to ask yourself: "Is my inner child desperate for some attention?"

To approach rebuilding a connection with your inner child, view this precious creature as an entity that deserves your unconditional love and protection. Acknowledge their pain, recognize how that pain manifests itself, and identify the unmet needs that are behind your triggers, negative behaviors, and hurt feelings.

Draw your inner child here:

Write It Out

Imagine yourself as your inner child's caretaker, the person that they need the most. The person who gets to heal and "save" them from feeling lost and disconnected. Which qualities and characteristics would you bring to the table to nurture this little bundle of chaos in order to reconnect with them and cultivate their joy? Are you patient? Affirming? Nurturing?

Reflect on these qualities and characteristics that you would use to help your inner child:

_____

Although you cannot go back and *change* your experiences or how you were cared for as a child, you *can* recognize that attempts to heal in forward motion can have the mysterious effect of rippling big healing through your perceptions of the past. This is powerful work, and it helps form the foundation of healing that can carry forward through future generations.

Unfortunately, in many cases, people are unconsciously bringing the same kind of neglect, judgment, and dismissive vibe to their inner child's cries for help as those same people were given as youngsters. It's time to stop that shit! If your inner child was *your* child, how well would you be caring for them? What kind of "reparenting" would you be giving them?

You have so much power over not only your shadows, but your healing as well. You can mourn the things that occurred in your past, and grieve the support you may have lacked, or the circumstances into which you were born. But in order to take control of the here and now, you must take responsibility for the road forward. It's time to take that inner child out of the shadow dungeon, give it some crayons or a nice run in the sunlight, and allow yourself to recognize that it has been a dear and darling part of you all along!

As with all shadow work efforts, it's important to note that the point of uncovering how you may or may not be repressing or putting aside your inner child is not to feel more guilt, shame, or icky feelings. The point is to recognize how deep the programming goes, take a deep fucking breath, and choose to move forward in a more empowered way. Guilt and shame are the least helpful tools in your arsenal when it comes to shadow work, as you cannot fight bad feelings with more of the same. (More on guilt and shame later.)

The following inner child prompt is designed to help you actively choose your reparenting strategies moving forward.

Fill It Out

Visualize standing before your inner child (the image you drew in the Draw It Out prompt in this chapter). With this image in mind, fill in the blanks in the following statements as a commitment to integrating your inner child into your larger awareness and healing efforts. You will do the work of integration in Phase 3 of this book, but this self-commitment is a great way to prep for that practice.

Fill in the blanks and speak to your inner child:

Although you may have felt _____ in the past,

I commit to bringing you a fuck-ton of love, _____,

and _____ in order for you to feel safe and whole.

When you act out or cry for help by_____,
I commit to attending to you with acceptance and care.

I appreciate the_____ burrowed within you,
and look forward to coaxing our light out, together.

Love, _____

    This whole exercise must be done in the spirit of radical acceptance and zero judgment! This is the kind of unconditional, fuckery-free love that your inner child needs most. And the more this part of you gets integrated into the wholeness of who you are, the more you will feel nurtured—and safe to tap back into a sense of wonder and childlike joy whenever the mood strikes.

⧚ Integration Tip

Although we are conceptualizing parts of the shadow from a "third party" perspective to help us in Phases 1 and 2 of shadow work, the secret to integration will always be in recognizing that these aspects are *not* outside of the self, but a part of it. This will be a larger part of the integration phase of this workbook. For Phases 1 and 2, viewing your shadow pieces (such as the inner child) as outside entities to get to know them more deeply is a helpful part of the process.

Chapter 6

Keeping Score
Challenging Envy and Judgment

One of the most common ways we can perceive the shadow in action is when the "green-eyed monster" enters the picture. Jealousy and envy, while normal human emotions, can sometimes surprise us with when and how they pop in to steal the show.

Think It Out

Reflect on some of the following common areas of life that can elicit jealousy or envy in people. Feel free to check the ones you're experienced with, and add your own.

- ☐ Career
- ☐ Academics/intellect
- ☐ Material possessions
- ☐ Romance
- ☐ Finances

- ☐ Aesthetics
- ☐ Friendships
- ☐ _____
- ☐ _____
- ☐ _____

Although envy and jealousy can take root in similar shadowy wounds, there's differences between the two that are important to understand, particularly when exploring these issues in the context of challenging and shifting these feelings.

If envy is the urge to peek at someone else's plate to covet the things that are there, jealousy is when you clutch your own plate (or the things you *already* possess) with white-knuckled vigilance in the fear that someone else could attempt to take it from you. So while jealousy could certainly be considered a subtype of envy, you can see how jealousy and envy may be cases where different exposed nerves are being hit, and different roots and shadowy cores are attached. Understanding how both or either of these feelings manifest in your life will be key to bringing them to light and accepting these murkier parts of yourself.

Let's start with envy. Envy is a normal and sometimes even functional behavior and response in the human species. It can help you get clarity on what you do and do not want, and it can sometimes inspire motivation for improving your circumstances. However, the feeling of envy is typically an unpleasant one, characterized by a sense of longing or resentment, and when it leaks out in ways that are dysfunctional, rude, or in conflict with your values, you can get startled by its shadowy presence.

Nobody wants to be a hater, but sometimes your shadow can be the hater within!

Envy can be a lot easier to overlook when it is directed toward things that are outside of your immediate circle of life. The burst of envy you might get when watching the seemingly glittery lives of the rich and famous usually won't lead to any cognitive dissonance. But when envy pops up triggered by the blessings or circumstances of those you are genuinely rooting for (like friends and family), you can get a keen sense that there are parts of you that you maybe wish could stay a little more hidden a little longer!

⚡ Integration Tip

Cognitive dissonance is that weird mental fun house feeling you get when you become aware that your behavior does not match what you consciously think you feel (your values). This is important to understand for shadow integration, because it can cause you to engage in some mental and emotional gymnastics to reduce the feeling of conflict. To bring it into conscious awareness, acknowledge its presence and allow yourself to explore what's at the root of the contradiction.

Picture this, for instance: A coworker you are friends with gets a promotion that you were really hoping for. Although you are happy for and proud of them, you find yourself blindsided by a lot of shitty feelings about your friend and the situation in general. This is the perception piece of the shadow work journey, and the more bad vibes you feel toward the other person or situation, the worse you feel about yourself. You may find yourself thinking, *Why am I feeling bitter, resentful, and envious of someone I care about and WANT to win?* This can trigger big feelings of guilt, shame, and an overwhelming desire to shut that shit down fast. Partly because the feelings are so uncomfortable, and partly out of the fear of coming across as an unsupportive asshole. In this example, the shadow self is throwing out undeniable proof that there is so much more going on in the psyche beyond conscious core values or ideas of who you truly are.

Again, you can't solve repression with more repression. You can't throw guilt or shame on negative feelings and expect that anything bright or light can blossom. Any attempts to gloss over or further repress this will likely result in it simmering like a resentful stew on the fringes of your awareness. Or even worse, the shadow can spread and leak out in unforeseen ways, such as sabotaging the job or relationship with your coworker (or both).

Write It Out

Reflect on a situation or circumstance where a feeling of envy popped up and surprised the shit out of you:

_____

_____

_____

_____

_____

_____

_____

_____

_____

_____

_____

Why was this situation so jarring? How did it conflict with the conscious version of yourself you thought you knew?

_____

_____

_____

_____

_____

_____

_____

_____

_____

_____

_____

With all inner demons, it's important to understand where they are coming from. Envy in particular tends to be the shadow franken-baby of comparison and _not enough-ness_. Like many (or most) shadows, it's really a response that emerges from a deeper root of what you subconsciously think of _yourself_. It's what happens when you subconsciously witness the circumstances happening outside of you, using what you see (which is also filtered through the lens of your subjective awareness, wounds, and all that fun stuff) to make inferences about what's _inside_ of you, and whether your own circumstances are fair, deserved, enough, etc. We will dig deeper into the root causes of emotions like envy in Phase 2.

When it comes to jealousy, there seems to be a similar component of insecurity and scarcity, but it can be more specifically touching on very negative beliefs about other people. Jealousy can often come with the idea that other people don't deserve what they have, or that they may have or take something that you may be telling yourself should be yours.

Feelings like envy and jealousy typically arise from a deep sense of lack, characterized by feelings of scarcity (the feeling that there isn't enough to go around), insecurity (uncertainty, anxiety, or threatened feelings about either your own qualities or what's available to you), and comparison (the age-old urge to peek at what's on someone else's paper in reference to your own). Despite best efforts to stabilize these emotions with logic, it can be just too tempting to your shadowy sides to peek at the things going on for those around you; it allows you to confirm your own beliefs about your inadequacies, the unfairness of life in general, or how you are cursed, overlooked, or chronically left behind.

Delicious, shadowy self-loathing!

Because envy and jealousy can leave a bad taste in your mouth and leave you feeling perpetually unfulfilled or bitter, it can be helpful to hone your awareness to take inventory of all you have in the spirit of gratitude. What things aren't you paying attention to that are good? You do indeed deserve them! While envy and jealousy are normal parts of the human emotional experience, recognizing their shadowy nature gives you a chance to see where work needs to be done so you can feel better within yourself, while also having the ability to put your best foot forward with others.

Write It Out

List some of the big and small blessings in your life:

_____

_____

_____

_____

_____

_____

_____

_____

_____

_____

_____

_____

_____

_____

_____

_____

_____

Now write down an affirmation statement about how you are worthy of the things you listed, regardless of any feelings of lack that may be lingering in your unconscious awareness.

For example: "I have many great and wonderful things surrounding me in my life, and they are a testament to the good things also within me. I am grateful for each of these blessings, and I am fully worthy of them."

_____

_____

_____

_____

_____

_____

Chapter 7

Behold! The Mirror
Judgment and Self-Concept

Despite the fact that we are unique and mysterious individuals, many of us humans operate in similar ways, and give off subtle tells about who we are and how we think. One of these tells lies in our judgments. Although it's a bit of a mindfuck, the things we judge about others is most often a glaring flag of what we think of *ourselves*. This is also true for the way we feel about the world around us.

Some examples of where a judgment can come from:

- People who judge those who express themselves freely may feel a deep unfairness that they themselves have repressed their own creative self-expression.

- People who judge those around them as thinking that they are superior ("You think you're better than me") are often masking deep insecurity.

- People who point fingers at others are often deeply unsure of their own virtues.

You see where I'm going here.

In spiritual circles you can often hear the phrase that the outside world and all the people in it are all a mirror. And while I think this is a bit of an oversimplification (some people don't trigger you because of your shadows; they are just objectively behaving like assholes), you do filter everything that you see and encounter through the subjective lens of your worldview, beliefs, and experiences. And you do so on both a conscious and an unconscious level. This is why two people can have the same interaction and interpret it dramatically differently from one another, depending on what their particular hang-ups and shadows may be.

⚡ Integration Tip

No discussion of the shadow would be complete without mentioning projection. Projection is the psychological phenomenon of assigning our own flaws to others rather than facing them within ourselves. It's an easy pattern to fall into, and many basic shadow work exercises call for looking at what you condemn in others as a starting point for acknowledging them as being a part of your inner makeup as well.

In most cases, the way you perceive yourself will be evident in the way you perceive the world. If you perceive yourself as unlovable or deeply inadequate, the world may seem more cruel and unjust toward you. If you judge others for being too soft, perhaps there is a softness in you that is neglected and in need of a space to be free. And so on.

The truth is that your opinion of yourself will be reflected back at you in both large and small ways as you move through life. And although your self-concept may have been shaped by the conditioning you picked up as a child, you undoubtedly have the power to turn that shit around at any point. And it starts with the perception phase of shadow work. As Stephen R. Covey says in his book *The 7 Habits of Highly Effective People: Powerful Lessons in Personal Change*, "We see the world, not as it is, but as we are—or, as we are conditioned to see it." Once you begin to monkey around with your self-concept on the shadow level, you're essentially building a stronger foundation to be the person you want to be.

As the first step, devote some time to simply observing yourself and your responses to the world around you. It is in this inquiry process that you can begin to see just what you're working with, regarding both self-concept and your larger perceptions of other people and the world at large.

Write It Out

Answer the following prompts to explore how you precieve yourself and the world you inhabit:

1. If you had to describe your self-concept, how would that look?

_____

_____

_____

_____

_____

2. What kind of outlook do you have? What evidence do you have to support or *not* support this outlook?

_____

_____

_____

_____

_____

3. What are your expectations, needs, and desires for life?

_____

_____

_____

_____

_____

4. To help the illumination process, it's also important to dig into your core values and the things that go against those ideals. What do you value and admire?

_____

_____

_____

_____

_____

5. What gives you the icks or a full-body "fuck no"? Acknowledging these dimensions in others can help you pull the thread of your self-concept.

_____

_____

_____

_____

_____

Fill It Out

If I had to pick three core values for myself, they would be:

1. _____ 2. _____ 3. _____

The three qualities I admire the most in other people include:

1. _____ 2. _____ 3. _____

I find these qualities valuable because _____
_____.

Being around people with those qualities makes me feel...
_____.

Pull the thread: Are you able to see yourself reflected in people with these qualities? In what ways?

_____

_____

_____

_____

The three qualities I do not like in others are:

1. _____ 2. _____ 3. _____

I find these qualities off-putting because _____
_____.

Being around people with those qualities makes me feel...

_____.

Pull the thread: Are you able to see yourself reflected in these qualities? In what ways?

_____

_____

_____

_____

An interesting side effect of shadow integration (and healing in general) is that when you step into your own confidence, power, and authenticity, the less likely it is that you will judge, be triggered easily by, or make inferences about other people's beliefs or motivations. This is why shadow work can not only be of benefit to your experience of life, but also to your *interpretation* of it. In understanding yourself better, you will be more understanding and accepting of others as well. A whole nuanced world of possibilities will open up, and you will find a wellspring of love, compassion, and understanding for both the light and shadow aspects that exist within you, and those that are reflected back to you. In Phase 3, integration and synthesis, you will be exploring this concept in more depth; however, it's important throughout every phase of shadow work that you keep your eyes on the prize: a life that's more intentional, authentic, and free!

Chapter 8

Beware! The Monster
Exploring Your Bad Behavior

While the majority of our work within this book thus far has been with some of the more tender aspects of the shadow that are hidden by way of social conditioning, fears, and traumas, no shadow work is complete without a deep dive into the more monstrous manifestations of it. Behaviors, urges, and feelings that reflect the ugliest representations of our repressed bad sides. It is here where we find our egos splitting and wanting to insert distance from the more embarrassing icks within ourselves—things like resentment, rage, bigotry, hate, control, pettiness, and greed. All the things we see in others but struggle to face within ourselves. These are just a few of the demons that can hide in the realm of the shadow.

It typically goes something like this: As you were growing up, you may have experimented with expressing some of these naughty tendencies, and found that doing so got a less-than-desirable result. Things like lying, cheating, or submitting to explosive anger were not only unhelpful, but may have gotten a response from your caregivers or peers that would have had you scrambling to cut that shit out and repress those nasty little tendencies in the future.

However, as you now know, repressing these things does not make them go away. Instead, a repressed shadow finds ways to emerge which can flat-out blindside you on a personal level. For instance, a repressed shadow of anger may come out unexpectedly toward a loved one who doesn't deserve it, or a repressed shadow that desires control may lead you to unconsciously dominate those around you.

That which you stuff down, unintegrated into the dungeon of your psyche, is that which will misbehave behind your back. And that which you deny is that which will fuck with you doubly. It is absolutely imperative that you take ownership of the kaleidoscopic multidimensional nature of who you are, and in doing so, take that first big step toward accepting that some of those dimensions are…well…kinda awful.

Draw It Out

It starts with acknowledging what these dimensions are. Can you admit to some of these demons that live within your own shadowy realms? Choose three that are the most prevalent for you, and try to draw them out as actual monsters. You don't need to be an artist, so have fun and explore how you're intuitively led to draw them. How big are they in relationship to each other? What are their features and characteristics?

When talking about the monsters within you, it's important to reflect on the fact that there is a collective shadow at play beyond the individual. Throughout history, many horrific atrocities have been committed that allow us in hindsight to take a peek into the collective shadow. Learning from this stuff comes not by distancing yourself from it, but by accepting that you may also hold the seeds within you to bear monstrous fruit. Across the board, it seems that humans are capable of a laundry list of fuckery where the shadow is involved; when we ignore or deny those qualities within us on an individual level, they can leak out, leading us to act in strange and terrible ways. For instance, there have been many examples throughout history of individuals doing harm when bolstered by the belief that they are doing good, doing the mental gymnastics necessary to protect their ego along the way. Again, you cannot fight repression with repression, and when you do, you can bet your ass that you'll find a hundred and one reasons why your crappy behavior is good, necessary, or justified.

If you're a human being, chances are you've had moments where you've let your lower self take the wheel. Maybe you've been blindsided by your own naughtiness? Really, would you even be a person if you didn't have a circumstance that made you feel wracked with guilt over acting like an insufferable asshole?!

In many cases this is how you can catch a glimpse of the parts of you that are typically repressed. When your values or ideas of who you are, are challenged by your own automatic responses or flared-up behaviors, your shadow has entered the chat. You may immediately self-soothe by shutting down the discomfort and cognitive dissonance that can emerge from these instances. It's time to roll up your sleeves and get your hands dirty instead.

Draw your monsters here:

Write It Out

Think of a time when you behaved in a way that was absolutely not in alignment with your values or ideas of who you are:

1. What was the situation?

_____

_____

_____

_____

_____

_____

_____

_____

2. How did you behave?

_____

_____

_____

_____

_____

_____

_____

_____

Reflect more on this disconnect between how you consciously viewed yourself and how you actually behaved:

_____

_____

_____

_____

_____

_____

_____

_____

_____

_____

_____

_____

_____

_____

_____

It is normal to feel shameful when reflecting on this kind of stuff, but the truth is that these things are learning experiences—inevitable collateral damage along your growth path. You can forgive yourself as a part of your shadow exploration. Recognize that just because someone may act shitty from time to time, doesn't mean they are a shitty person. Shadows such as greed, desires for power, manipulation, and the like are a part of life; why not love and accept the fact that while we are all kinda hardwired to be awful, more often than not people choose to be better? Great job!

The way the shadow manifests is often surprising, and it can be a tricky and elusive task to suss it out. The truth is that it takes determination to be able to take a cold hard look at the way you operate and take radical responsibility for it. For many people, instances of bad behavior can lead to feelings of denial, projection (blaming others), or even worse, helplessness (the idea that you have a shadow issue, but that you're powerless to change it).

However, if you really want to integrate these shadows into demons you can actually tame in the third phase of this work (integration), you'll need to have some difficult conversations with yourself about how these bad attitudes or poor behaviors might actually be fulfilling some need, or are potentially a manifestation of more vulnerable emotions, or "splitting" from the bits of yourself that you may struggle to love and accept. This will be explored more in Phase 2, the investigation phase of shadow work. Here, you may find, for example, rage or explosive anger may be hiding the vulnerability of fear or sadness, or it may be a way of feeling some sense of power and control when those things seem to be in short supply. Greed may be serving the purpose of soothing deep core wounds of scarcity. And "othering," or discriminating against people who are different than you, may serve to lull a deep insecurity in yourself, making you feel better than others—even if just for a moment. When you begin to see these things manifest in your life in the perception phase of shadow work, you are being given an invitation to unravel these threads.

Again, exploring your own inner demons means digging deep and getting those hands dirty: By being up to the challenge, you're further ahead than most!

Write It Out

Now it's your turn. Reflect on the demons you drew earlier in this chapter. Decide whether you want to stick to these three for this next prompt or revise them. Get playful and start a dialogue with them. Make friends with your demons by trying to understand them!

Use this space or a separate journal to answer the following questions and explore your demons further:

1. How may these demons be serving me?

_____

_____

_____

_____

_____

_____

2. Are they "messengers" for some other more vulnerable emotion?

○ Yes ○ No

If yes, explore these emotions:

_____

_____

_____

_____

_____

_____

Integration Tip

Take back the reins by acknowledging each of these demons and thanking them for their service. Try and think of how they have manifested in your life and reactions so far, and how you want to work with them moving forward. In the previous example of rage or explosive anger, for instance, you may turn your healing efforts to learning to identify and safely express other emotions so that they aren't turning into secondary anger. Or you may seek opportunities to add more structure and routine to what you *are* able to control, so that you are creating a sense of safety and security and diminishing your psyche's need to create these things through maladaptive means.

Chapter 9

Beloved! The Wounded
Feeling Your Missing Pieces

Although the concept of the shadow self most often conjures up mental notions of spooky darkness and nasty little demons within (as discussed in the previous chapter), you may be catching on to the trend that the shadow realms within us can also hold the bits of us we've lost along the way. Particularly in cases of deep traumas and pervasive wounds, the shadow can hold beautiful and light elements of ourselves, in a space that can feel so disconnected it can seem downright out of reach. In many cases, these parts were cast out from our awareness due to shame, trauma, self-preservation, or a deep desire to fit in.

These pieces of ourselves may include:

- Joy
- Creativity
- Authentic self-expression
- The ability to take risks
- Carefree optimism
- Pride and self-trust
- Confidence

There are many circumstances or triggers that can lead to an exploration of the shadow, but one for certain is a desire to get back to authenticity and true happiness—a sacred quest to find your "sparkle."

Sound familiar?

The good news is that you wouldn't feel such a keen desire to get back to a more balanced state if it wasn't both *possible* and *achievable*.

It may take some work, sure, but it's important to remember that many of the things that feel the most off-limits are the things people gatekeep mainly from *themselves*. The fact that you can sense the lack of these more carefree and positive elements of your personality just goes to show that you are sensing a disharmony (or dis-ease) in what should be your most natural and balanced state.

Write It Out

Answer the following questions to explore aspects of your personality you may be repressing:

1. What are some positive elements and characteristics that feel off-limits for you?

_____

_____

_____

_____

_____

2. How do you feel about yourself?

_____

_____

_____

_____

_____

When aspects of the personality that would be useful or beneficial are repressed, you can spend a lifetime longing to find the missing pieces. You may feel an overall sense of dissatisfaction, given the fact that part of your personality might feel off-limits. This is the awareness of a kind of inauthenticity, one that feeds into destabilization, feelings of impostor syndrome, and a lack of self-trust across the board. You can probably see how this quickly becomes a spiral that causes more of the same, leading to broad overgeneralizations that perhaps you are broken, lost, or utterly unable to be fixed.

Breathe, baby!

The truth is that the accumulation of any person's shadow aspects is a dynamic process that's influenced by a lot of shit. There may be elements of individual temperament, genetics, family dynamics, subtle and not-so-subtle programming, the influence of the collective, the social dynamics experienced, traumatic and mundane events—truly the list is endless. When it comes to the shadow, we are all a perfect storm of nature and nurture—dynamic, puzzling, and beautifully, bewilderingly complex.

The following is a list of scenes and scenarios where you can perceive that the light has been held hostage by the shadow. To give some context, each includes a brief description of how this repression of what Jung referred to as the "golden shadow" may have occurred. (You will explore in more depth how these things occur in Phase 2 of this workbook.)

- A person who struggles to let their creativity loose may have been a child who was often told to quiet down by their parents or ridiculed by their peers.

- A person who struggles with their confidence may have had their outward displays of confidence squashed in the past, leading to a deep sense of shame and self-correction to repress their confident side.

- Those who struggle to connect to their optimism and joy may have learned to repress these qualities to "fit in" with prevailing complaint culture.

- A person who represses their quirky authentic personality may have grown up being told they were "too much."

You get the drift.

In many cases, these light aspects that have been held back from you leave a void you fill with heavy feelings. The resulting burdens feel like lack, insecurity, confusion, shame, and an utter sense of unfulfillment.

Write It Out

Can you think of any examples like the ones outlined previously, where positive and authentic bits of you might be held back in the shadow?

The good news is that all of these aspects are inside you just waiting to be set free again. Personal development in this realm isn't development at all. It is more of a reclamation, a return to who the most natural and authentic expression of you deeply desires to be. At any given point, you have the ability to decide to shift the narrative *just because you can.* This requires only a few things from you…

First, you will need to align your own personal energy behind the moves you make. If you are straight with yourself, then fears about judgments from the outside wouldn't even come into play. The truth is that people only worry about how others are gonna receive them when they are judging themselves. You are your original gatekeeper.

Next, you will need to take a fine-tooth comb to your programming, worldview, and belief systems to pluck out the bullshit like you'd pluck out a nasty case of lice. Do you truly believe the shit you believe, or are you holding on to a big ol' bag of smoldering nonsense that others gave you? Many people live their whole lives without daring to rock the boat of their own beliefs. However, in most cases it only takes a couple of journal prompts to send yourself into a tailspin of cognitive dissonance that can inspire years of chain-breaking and an illuminating courtship with the self. Just having your nose in this very book is a cobblestone on this path.

And finally, you will need to be ready to be brutally honest with yourself about whether you're standing in your own way. As was touched on before, many shadows are misguided elements of the psyche trying to nurture or protect you. Can you have a heart-to-heart with yourself and recognize why it feels darkly soothing to tell yourself things like, "I'm never going to be confident," "I'm worthless," or "I don't have an authentic personality"? Are you ready to take these steps in Phases 2 and 3 of your shadow work to open the gates and change the narrative, even if it means holding new beliefs in your heart when challenged with situations that feed the old beliefs?

Write It Out

Explore the following questions to dig deeper into releasing your authentic self:

1. What are you ready to set free?

_____

_____

_____

_____

2. What light aspects are you ready to integrate back into your outward expression?

_____

_____

_____

_____

⚡ Integration Tip

Take some of these missing-piece qualities and meditate on each one individually. What sensations arise in your body? Where do you feel them? Is there any mental resistance or specific thoughts that come when reflecting on these? Associated memories? To integrate these back into your conscious awareness, you need to accept that they are a part of you. Lovingly. For example, if creative self-expression is one of your pieces of light, meditate on that concept and allow yourself to connect to it emotionally. If it feels a little out of reach, it can be helpful to remember when you last felt that sense of creative self-expression, as a way to anchor in the feeling. Practice letting yourself feel the presence of these qualities until doing so begins to feel more natural.

Write yourself a letter of loving permission to be unapologetically yourself. Keep this letter in mind as you move through Phases 2 and 3 of this workbook.

Dear _____ ,

_____

_____

_____

_____

_____

_____

_____

_____

_____

_____

_____

_____

_____

_____

_____

_____

_____

_____

_____

_____

Love, _____

Chapter 10

The Shame Game
Looking Deeper at Guilt, Shame, and Fear

As hard as it may be to admit, many of us have an addiction to the help-lessness and self-confirming bullshit that comes with emotions such as guilt, shame, and fear. Although we don't *consciously enjoy* these feelings or the havoc they wreak in our lives, many of them fill shadowy needs for us; otherwise, we'd probably have a simpler time letting them go! The truth about our shadows is that many of them have deep tangling tap-roots in shame and fear. These themes can disguise themselves as other emotions, manifesting in surprising and sometimes agonizing ways.

Although guilt and shame are often thought of in association with one another, they are different. In order to get to know them better, it's important to first understand and respect them as distinct creatures.

Guilt is a feeling like you fucked up. Although not a pleasant feeling, it is one that is adaptive, since it can help keep you on the straight and narrow. Guilt can pop up in your awareness in a variety of ways including denial, self-flagellation, or the chronic urge to do too much.

A feeling of guilt is usually easy to associate with a certain event or thing (for example, "I did XYZ and now I feel like shit"). Although guilt is a type of mental distress, it can also cause troubling physical symptoms that can be hard to ignore, such as stomach upset, anxious jitters, and interruption in breathing patterns.

Guilt, like pain, can be a firm but fair "Fuck your feelings" kind of teacher. It has the energy of a grandmother who genuinely has your best interests at heart, but who isn't afraid to help you find out should you care to fuck around! As a prosocial species, people literally evolved and adapted to have a moral compass and a strong sense of values that correlate to the good of the community. In this way, guilt can be adaptive, as everyone is apt to slip up and act like the flawed human they are. Both the mental and physiological symptoms of guilt can act as a course corrector that can allow you to grow and evolve into a version of yourself that is constantly learning to minimize the discomfort felt when behaving in ways that aren't integral to who you think you are or who you want to be.

The thing about guilt, however, is that it's only helpful to a point. Beyond a certain curve in the road, it just becomes a way for your shadow to writhe around in indulgent, masochistic penance. The shadow can use guilt as an "in" to express itself in a spectrum of ways that range from a denial/repression of guilty feelings themselves (and you bet your sweet ass they will leak out somehow, some way, typically in the form of projection) to a full-on rager of a pity party that lets a person wear and reexperience their guilt like a perfume a lover might don as a signature scent. In the latter example, this shadowy tendency to latch onto guilt as some sort of self-confirming evidence of inherent "badness" gives some insight on the connection between guilt and shame.

Shame can have the same oppressively awful feeling as guilt. However, instead of this emotion being tied to a certain action or concrete trigger, it's more about *who you feel you are*. There is a complex and dynamic relationship between shame, unworthiness, and the overwhelming feeling that who you are on the deepest level is not much more than a problem that needs to be fixed.

If only this wasn't so damn relatable!

Shame leads down dark paths that put inner peace and sometimes even physical well-being at risk. Chapter 7 talked about the impact of self-concept on how you experience the world and what you accept from it. Shame, or a feeling that there is something deeply wrong or awful about you (not tied to a specific moral event, just a general sense of "badness" or brokenness), can lead people to strive for perfection that doesn't exist, making them behave in ways that are reckless toward their own health and well-being. It can also lead to trash-talking themselves and subconsciously holding themselves off from things that are good for them or bring them joy.

Your shadow will gatekeep your success, happiness, and potential in ways that outside forces could never pull off. Shame plays a huge role in the kind of self-sabotage seen in the shadow realms, as all people will subconsciously operate in a way that gives them what they feel they deserve.

As part of the illumination process, the deep roots of shame and how they were planted must be understood. We will dive into this further in Phase 2, but it's important to note that in many cases, shame arises from traumas and childhood wounds that had to do with getting your needs met. Many people who have deep-rooted shame shadows also have a history of swallowing their own needs and emotions to help keep those around them stable. There can also be a common thread of traumatic events and abuses that managed to pull the rug out from under a person at a young age, leaving a sensation of a lack of safety or disconnection between how they viewed others and how they viewed themselves. These experiences can form the kinds of pervasive patterns that you see in the perception phase of shadow work.

Write It Out

Try to think of three core memories that involve the feeling of shame. I mean, the kind of experiences that you think of at 2 a.m. when you can't sleep because your brain decides to torture you.

Fill out the following exploration process for each of these experiences, either in the space provided or in a separate journal:

1. Core memory:

_____

_____

- Scene setting and circumstances (i.e., what happened):

  _____

  _____

  _____

  _____

- Your mental, emotional, and physical response to what happened (you may even tap into this response again now while simply reflecting on this event):

  _____

  _____

  _____

  _____

- Belief(s) that this situation exposes or contributes to (e.g., I am not safe to speak up; I do not fit in with other people):

  _____

  _____

  _____

  _____

2. Core memory:

_____

_____

- Scene setting and circumstances (i.e., what happened):

  _____

  _____

  _____

  _____

- Your mental, emotional, and physical response to what happened (you may even tap into this response again now while simply reflecting on this event):

  _____

  _____

  _____

  _____

- Belief(s) that this situation exposes or contributes to (e.g., I am not safe to speak up; I do not fit in with other people):

  _____

  _____

  _____

  _____

3. Core memory:

_____

_____

- Scene setting and circumstances (i.e., what happened):

  _____

  _____

  _____

  _____

- Your mental, emotional, and physical response to what happened (you may even tap into this response again now while simply reflecting on this event):

  _____

  _____

  _____

  _____

- Belief(s) that this situation exposes or contributes to (e.g., I am not safe to speak up; I do not fit in with other people):

  _____

  _____

  _____

  _____

Now, no conversation about guilt and shame in the context of the shadow would be complete without acknowledging the presence of fear. This workbook previously covered the basics of fear and the many ways that it feeds and contributes to the shadow. It is no different when talking about shame and unworthiness, as you may hold a secret fear that not only are you inherently bad and broken (this may even feel like an accepted "fact" for some), but you may deeply fear disappointing others or having others find out how totally and utterly messed up you might feel yourself to be. This in and of itself can be a mighty thread to begin unraveling, so let's take a moment to explore the role of fear and how it connects to guilt and shame.

⚡ Integration Tip

In many cases, shameful feelings are shaped by the response you received from the environment around you. When looking at the difference between the average child and the average adult, you can clearly see that shame is something that is adopted along the way, not something people are inherently born with. In order to transmute or clear deep feelings of shame, you need to critically analyze the contexts you developed in. For example, if your feelings of shame came from the messages you got from someone who was abusive or full of shame themselves, would this be the most reliable source to learn from? Although you cannot change the hands of fate that you were dealt in the past, you can take personal responsibility to commit to providing a new narrative if the ones you were given were shit.

Write It Out

Freewriting is a process of simply putting pen to paper and allowing what needs to come out to come out! Let yourself freewrite using what you have learned in this chapter about guilt and shame to help in this prompt.

Freewrite in the space provided about the role of fear in your life, relationships, and self-concept as it relates to guilt and shame:

_____

_____

_____

_____

_____

_____

_____

_____

_____

_____

_____

Some of the things that you've freewritten here may give you an intuitive sense of what needs deeper exploration. You will know as you freely write what is a "good lead" for further exploration, as you will likely feel it in your body or have associated memories brought up. It's important to remind yourself that fear is a normal part of the human emotional system, but not always necessarily an accurate representation of reality. In many cases, these fears are old programming picked up from outside yourself and codified as law by your shadows. Usually when bad stuff actually happens, it is less distressing and dramatic than what you may have imagined through the lens of fear.

Chapter 11

Playing Your Role
Investigating Your Relationships with Other People

Although we looked at the tendency to fall into certain patterns and roles in our relationships with others earlier in this workbook, it's worth delving into further. Relationships can act as a shadow playground, a place for all of our wounds, projections, and maladaptive comfort patterns to come out and play!

Despite even the best efforts to approach life in a conscious and healthy way, our subconscious is like a hidden control room that can influence various dimensions of life in a pretty profound way. And interpersonal relationships are one of these dimensions where the shadow can rear its ugly head in both big and small ways. Shadow work isn't *just* for personal improvement; it can dramatically shift the level to which you are able to connect with others. For example, it can:

- Improve your self-awareness so you don't act up then turn around and play the blame game with others.

- Help you have a better ability to understand other people, holding space for the fact that they might be operating from their own shadowy wounds as well.

- Help you to cut the unhealed bullshit and communicate better with others.

Earlier in this phase, you explored the sneaky ways in which your shadows can be seen in the patterns you end up in, and in the sneaky ways in which you may self-sabotage. Similarly, many people can find themselves magnetizing to certain types of people who fill in for their shadows and wage war on their peace. For example, a person may:

- Be attracted to people who treat them poorly to confirm the inner beliefs they have that they are unworthy and unlovable.

- Give their shadows the wheel when faced with deep fears and insecurities, and this can fulfill the prophecy that they can't have meaningful relationships.

- Hold others responsible for their healing or happiness—something that is never gonna work and will leave them feeling worse than they started 100 percent of the time.

- Allow themselves to be controlled or dominated even if they consciously hate it, because they don't fully trust themselves to make the right moves.

- Become attracted to toxic forms of love like possessiveness and control because they can fulfill shadowy desires for love and attention.

And so on. In fact, every toxic relationship seems to be based more on shadow interference than genuine conscious love. Although there may be good intentions and love in the mix, a healthy foundation of genuine love and care is only possible if both parties take seriously the responsibility of making themselves whole; otherwise they risk falling into traps of codependency, chaos, and abuse.

That being said, it's important to note that not all of these interpersonal relationships are romantic. There are a variety of shadowy dynamics and patterns that can come up within families, with friends and coworkers, and more.

Before carrying on, it might be worth taking a little snapshot of your interpersonal life in order to get some clarity on what particular issues you can identify straight off the hop.

Talk It Out

Set yourself up across from an empty space or a mirror, and explore the following questions aloud, letting yourself answer honestly, impulsively, and without rehearsal. Your answers should be a kind of "free association" and can be as long or as short as you please. The important thing is to just talk these things through aloud as far as they will take you. Feel free to write out any aha moments you had afterward.

Talk with your shadow, and ask them the following questions:

1. How do you feel about other people and interpersonal relationships? These can be familiar, platonic, or even romantic. You may find that one certain dimension or type of relationship inspires more to talk about.

2. How do you feel these beliefs are reflected in your current reality and interpersonal relationships?

Your shadows can be seen not only in the type and quality of relationships you engage in, but also in the kind of behaviors you exhibit or tolerate in these relationships. Usually these can be seen as a reflection of your shadowy beliefs, and the core wounds (more on this in Phase 2) deep at the heart of them. This can form the foundation for shadowy behaviors such as jealousy in relationships, the fear of making friends (or a habit of pushing friends away), a tendency to overexplain yourself in order to be understood, or generally taking on the least charitable way of understanding the behaviors of others in times of conflict.

Other shadowy behaviors in any kind of relationship include:

- Manipulation or lying
- Fawning (or excessive flattery)
- Insecurity (e.g., attention-seeking)
- Passive-aggression
- Boundary-pushing
- "Ghosting" people
- "Losing" yourself or your identity in relationships

Fill It Out

For the following prompt, fill in the blanks with a word or short phrase that explains how you feel when it comes to other people and your interpersonal relationships. If any of these require more thread-pulling or exploration, feel free to write it out in the white space of this workbook or in a separate journal.

Fill in the blanks to explore your feelings about relationships:

In general, I feel that other people are _____ .

I feel _____ about getting into new relationships.

Romantic relationships typically make me feel _____ .

I get _____ feelings about making new friends.

When I meet new people, I hope the impression they get of me is:

_____

_____

Qualities I look for in new platonic and romantic relationships include:

_____

_____

In my interactions with other people, I typically find myself in the role of

_____ . I feel _____ about that recurring experience.

⚡ Integration Tip

If we can get to a place of lovingly calling ourselves out for being clingy, inauthentic, controlling, distrustful, etc., then we can truly say we are doing the work to illuminate our shadows. After all, integration is becoming whole—being a sum of the good, the bad, *and* the ugly. It's okay: We all act a little shitty, and it's a good example of the kind of repression that's enforced on the collective level. Nobody (at least, almost nobody) wants to be an asshole, and yet we all have an asshole within. So if you're truly wanting to heal in the realm of interpersonal shadows, ask yourself the hard questions like, "Am I the asshole here?" Allow yourself to be humbled and gently course-correct when the answer is yes.

Write It Out

To continue digging into your interpersonal shadows, try out the following writing prompt. Here, you'll find a list of different shadowy aspects of relationships.

Check all the ones that you can identify as being part of your own interpersonal relationship style at times. It's okay if you check them all, I certainly could….After all, we're only human!

- ☐ Dismissive
- ☐ Inconsiderate
- ☐ Controlling
- ☐ Guarded or distrustful
- ☐ Attention-seeking
- ☐ Jealous
- ☐ Clingy
- ☐ Helpless
- ☐ Passive-aggressive
- ☐ Angry
- ☐ Score-keeping

If you can recognize these as shadows that are present in your life, a little reprogramming is all that may be needed to shift the narrative. It might be as simple as telling yourself, "I noticed XYZ pattern, and I am ready to call in a new dynamic because I deserve something more supportive to me." You will practice shifting the narrative in Phase 3 of this workbook.

As you illuminate your shadows, the quality and caliber of your relationships can naturally start to change, because you begin to conduct yourself differently, and practice loving yourself enough to recognize shadowy behaviors in others as well. This is why you may have heard about people losing certain relationships when they begin healing. They no longer tolerate bullshit, or they find themselves on such a different level that it becomes hard to relate to those who are not working to heal themselves.

Reflect on the characteristics that you identified:

_____

_____

_____

_____

_____

_____

_____

_____

_____

_____

Phase Two

INVESTIGATION
Getting Cozy with Your Shadow

Now that we've explored the many ways in which our shadows can manifest in our conscious lives, it's time to move on to the phase of shadow work that consists of sifting further through these murky aspects. This is the part where we grab our demons, sit them down, and ask, "Baby, who hurt you?"

In the following chapters, you will begin to delve into the roots of your shadows. The investigation process here is a focused attempt at inquiry and self-reflection. How did your shadows develop, and where did they come from? Is it possible they are serving you or helping you? What needs are they trying to fulfill? How did they come to join you across the lifespan? Although some of these questions came up in Phase 1, here you will dig deeper.

This part is full of prompts and techniques for understanding and reflecting on your shadows and how they've developed and become part of your cabinet of repression. This phase of the work will be tackled not only with journal prompts (much like the illumination and reflection questions throughout this workbook), but also with creation, meditation, and visioning processes. You'll reconceptualize the past, discover core wounds, craft a body map to learn the somatic component to shadows, and more!

Self-understanding is needed for integration. However, due to the fact that shadows can be tricky, it can help at this phase of the process to "outsource" your shadows, or look at them as outside entities, in order to consider different possibilities and interpretations. Picture it this way: If you need to fix a car, you may have to remove the piece(s) that isn't working from the car to get a full view of it from all sides and understand the different things that may be at play and how they are affecting the car.

So get ready to examine your shadows with the curiosity of a detective inspecting clues for their deeper meaning. In doing so you can learn their processes and vulnerabilities and build self-compassion that will help you in Phase 3 as you work to accept your shadows as part of who you are.

Chapter 12

When Actions Speak Louder Than Words
Understanding the Functions of Shadowy Behavior

Back before I ditched the nine-to-five to live a life of reckless creation, I worked in community inclusion, and a lot of my job revolved around behavioral supports and alternative modes of communication. My education and experience in this work was transformational not only for my career, but also for approaching my own painfully human personal life. It was here that I learned the power of behavior as a form of functional communication, something that has stuck with me ever since.

The knowledge that many of the bewildering things that you, and I, and other humans do may somehow be serving a purpose or filling a need is both intriguing and liberating!

In my inclusion work, I had to maintain a keen understanding of the functions of behavior in order to be able to successfully support those who may not have had the communication tools to explain their needs. When learning all of this, it struck me as odd that not everyone is equipped with this knowledge, as the world would likely be a lot more understanding and compassionate if that was so! Certainly this is relevant for parenting; however, it's fucking awesome whether you're dealing with a customer, a partner, or a friend as well. There are really no limits to how this understanding will drastically change your perspective. The four basic functions of behavior are:

1. **Attention:** Getting some sort of praise or social reward in the form of attention.

2. **Escape:** Avoidance or the removal of a situation or particularly uncomfortable or unpleasant thing.

3. **Access to tangible things:** Getting or obtaining actual items or things (either wanted or needed).

4. **Sensory stimulation:** Being stimulated in a sensory way (we do require this, after all!).

In the context of shadow work and integration, understanding that behavior has four basic functions is *huge*, because you can then see that:

- A person who is perpetually in their victimhood shadow may be receiving attention or compassion from other people in a steady, addictive drip.

- A person who is constantly blowing up in anger to avoid uncomfortable conversations may be enacting a cycle of avoidance.

- A person who may have grown up in survival mode may play whatever role is required in a relationship to get access to tangible things like housing, necessities, etc.

- A person who may unexpectedly blow up their life or do seemingly crazy self-destructive things may be subconsciously rebelling against a feeling of depression and numbing out.

These are only a few examples, but they allow you to see that your shadowy behaviors don't come from a place of malice in most places. They are misguided attempts to get your needs met. This is why viewing them as "bad" or "good" is fundamentally incorrect.

⚡ Integration Tip

It's important for integration to really drive the point home that your ego and shadows ultimately have always been somewhat working *for* you, albeit in a very messy, uncoordinated, and ultimately largely impractical/unhelpful way. Once you detach from feeling negatively about yourself about this and accepting that this is a functional way that your subconscious goes about fulfilling your needs—keeping you safe, minimizing your discomfort, assuaging your fears, and more—you can let yourself really look at the root of what's happening with compassion and curiosity.

From a shadow work perspective, viewing the world through this lens can help you not take the behavior of others so personally, and find ways to understand your own behavior with compassion. Would you approach a wounded animal with angry, judgmental vibes? Would you attack a child for not behaving like a fully grown well-adjusted adult? You deserve all the same kind of understanding and grace you would give anybody else. In many cases, you might be better off *thanking* your shadow for getting needs met that your conscious awareness couldn't.

Write It Out

Can you take a hard look at some of the ways your shadows are manifesting in your life and examine them through the lens of serving one or more of the four basic functions of behavior? Write them down.

Reflect on behavior you have experienced in each function:

1. Attention:

_____

_____

_____

2. Escape:

_____

_____

_____

3. Access to tangible things:

_____

_____

_____

4. Sensory stimulation:

_____

_____

_____

Again, not every shadowy behavior will be easily identifiable within this framework. However, all shadow work is undertaken with the hope of the ultimate payoff: lasting integration. And if you want to bring your shadows into your conscious awareness and learn how to navigate their influence in your life, understanding their function is going to be key.

In Phase 1 of this workbook you looked at the repeating patterns that manifest in your life due to the things that you are repressing. When you bring in the concept of behavior as communication in the investigation phase of this work, you may learn some deep uncomfortable truths. You may learn that some of these patterns are based on your subconscious trying to communicate with you. You may find that broken relationships take root in cycles of avoidance, or you may find that some of the poor choices you've made in the past were due to a deep desire for stimulation in some way, your shadow's way of shaking you awake.

Don't get it twisted: Your shadow and your ego have been a team, long before you even started the messy work of illumination and integration. The purpose of shadow work is to make that relationship more functional for your benefit—instead of their acting like shared custody parents that can't even be present in the same room, sneakily sabotaging each other. Training your awareness to look for the function of behavior allows you to take the first steps to do just that.

Phase 3 of this workbook will go over how this knowledge, in tandem with your knowledge of your unique triggers and core wounds, can help you to set yourself up for success, but for now just marinade on this concept of behavior as functional communication and how it may have been popping up in your life so far. For the next activity, revisit the questions earlier in this chapter about the different functions of behavior and how they manifest in your life. Can you pull those threads a little further to see when these patterns may have started?

Write It Out

Explore the root of any shadows you identified earlier that may be manifesting in the following ways. Try and think back to when you may have first noticed this pattern start up in your life, and in which ways you may have been lacking these elements.

Reflect on the root of the patterns you have identified in each:

1. Attention:

_____

_____

_____

2. Escape:

_____

_____

_____

3. Access to tangible things:

_____

_____

_____

4. Sensory stimulation:

_____

_____

_____

As you move forward through the following chapters, keep this in your mind, particularly when you revisit this topic in Phase 3. And above all else, recognize that no matter what you may be feeling guilty or weird about when it comes to shadowy behavior, everyone is having a chaotic and imperfect human experience, and there is nothing abnormal or strange about any of it—even the stuff you may not like. Coming to an understanding of how your behavior may be serving a function helps to really anchor that truth!

Chapter 13

Where Are You Going?
Creating a Life Map

Empowerment is a core motivation for getting into shadow work. By making your formerly hidden shadowy sides conscious, you can unlock a lot of freedom! Freedom from your own programming, freedom from the feeling of being "stuck," and freedom from being held back by self-sabotage and bullshit. The more you bring your metaphorical demons to the light and uproot dated beliefs, the more you can truly get to know the ins and outs of some of the dysfunction and drama in your life!

This is how you take your power back.

It's important to remember that you are both the creator and the main character in your life. Although life is shaped by a variety of outside influences and circumstances wholly beyond your control, there is a lot that you *can* choose that can course-correct in a big way. You are highly influential over your own life experience in so many ways. There is nobody else who has the power over your decisions, desires, and the mundane details of your day-to-day other than you. Although this is a mildly terrifying responsibility, the thought of it should also light a fire under your ass to take back the reins of your experiences, so you can navigate the things you've uncovered so far in this workbook and direct your path for the future.

Since this is the phase where you dig deeper into your shadows, a proper zoom out is helpful in order to conceptualize the whole of where you've been and where you're going. Your shadows are a necessary part of the whole of who you are, and are often shaped by where you've been. As mentioned in previous chapters, most people live out certain themes whether they are aware of them or not. They have been wrangled into certain roles, whether they consented to it or not. Stories can be reframed, but only once we can conceptualize their current framing, and the beliefs and baggage that are propping that shit up.

In Chapter 4 you looked at life events through the lens of personal mythology and lore. To deepen this playful way of exploring your inner narrative, you can also map out the themes, patterns, and events that impacted you. It is a powerful way for you to get introspective and explore your life's narrative, through the archetypal patterns and roles that have shaped your identity. Ideally you can get a bird's-eye view of the development of your shadows here. Creating a life map can also help you look to your past with compassion and context (rather than getting stuck in the sluggish mental realm of feelings). This can then help you move forward in a more compassionate, accepting, and empowered way.

Map It Out

In this prompt, you will go through the steps of making a life map. Make sure to set aside some time for this, coming armed with your personal shadow work strategies, and listening to your body as you go. You will also want a separate piece of paper so you'll have plenty of room to draw. If you want to make this a more creative endeavor, collect some images, paints, or vision-boardy things to help you illustrate your map.

1. Start by drawing a horizontal line from birth until the present on your piece of paper. Divide this line into broader phases and/or stages that make sense to you (think developmental stages, "eras," or pre/post specific events, etc.). You can brainstorm some of these phases here or in a separate journal.

_____

_____

_____

2. On your line, plot out some key events or "eras" (phases) that made an impact in your life.

- What are the things that shaped or changed you?

_____

_____

_____

_____

_____

_____

- What were some formative events, big and small, positive and negative?

_____

_____

_____

_____

_____

_____

Remember, the things that come to mind do not have to make sense to anyone but you. Resist the urge to make sense of it, as life doesn't always make sense (certainly true for the shadowy emotional realms!).

3. Taking it further, reflect on these questions as you create your timeline.

- Were these events internal or external? Meaning, were they internal shifts or occurrences that happened due to outside influences?

    ○ Internal   ○ External

- How much control did you or did you not have over them?

_____

_____

_____

_____

_____

_____

4. Think back to the personal mythology and lore you uncovered earlier in this workbook. Where would some of the themes or patterns in your mythology and lore occur on your life map (an optimistically oblivious "fool's era," a dark night of the soul, times of embarking on the unknown, etc.)? Plot them out on your map.

In the next prompt, you'll use your map to dig deeper.

Write It Out

Once you have followed the steps to create your life map, zoom out and consider the personal transformations you've gone through, as marked on this map. Reflect on all the times that your life felt as if it were zigzagging, yet it brought you to the present. Add any significant shifts that you may have missed in the previous steps now that you are looking at it as a whole.

Take a moment here to reflect on how all of these moments influenced your identity and perspectives:

_____

_____

_____

_____

_____

_____

_____

_____

_____

_____

_____

_____

_____

_____

_____

_____

As stated before, feel free to transfer this info into a more creative format if it suits you. Once you have your information, you can remake this life map through collage, paint it out, or simply just leave it as a written diagram. The choice is yours.

⟲ Integration Tip

By making your life map you can get a bird's-eye view of the themes, patterns, and archetypal journeys in your life. If you notice some shadows popping up in either your attitude toward the things that have happened in your life, or the patterns/roles/ themes you identify, take some time to explore whether these themes are fulfilling a need or supporting you in some way, even if it's hard to admit. Perhaps by recognizing and acknowledging them you can craft a new narrative for the future.

Chapter 14

Your Inner Voice
Crafting Your Shadow Persona

Since the goal for dealing with your shadows is unconditional love and acceptance, it can sometimes help to view your shadows as something *outside* yourself before beginning the tricky task of full acceptance and integration. It's due to the very presence of these shadows that, for some of us, treating ourselves with compassion and grace can feel like a bit of a stretch. Outsourcing that shit, as if we are extending those kind feelings to something else, may feel somewhat more manageable for some.

A shadow persona is a creative representation of your shadow self. Some common shadow personas are the:

- **Inner Critic:** that voice inside that's constantly nitpicking everything you do.

- **Inner Child:** the sweet but sometimes unhinged little child within us all, discussed in more depth in Chapter 5.

- **Helpless Victim:** the part of you that feels like everything will always go wrong so there is no point in trying.

- **"I'm Scared So I'll Just Get Angry" Guy:** the angry part that is a cunning redirection of more vulnerable feelings.

Since many people just so happen to have a multitude of different characters in their shadows, this task can be approached almost as if writing a cast of characters for a fictional book or movie. Try picturing these characters and their unique "personas" in your mind, perhaps even thinking of real-life or fictional counterparts that you feel embody these personas.

Integration, or radical acceptance of *all* of these parts being a part of you, is by far the most important aspect of shadow work; it will lead to lasting change and healing. However, it is not possible to integrate something which you do not understand. For the illumination process, it is imperative to get crystal fucking clear with what you're dealing with.

Beyond shadow work alone, clarity is the number one tool that will help with any form of transformational healing. However, this requires moving beyond a surface-level speculation of what issues are present and how. Although there are many folks out there who recognize they have some shit to work on, only a small percentage of those will be moved to act on what to do with that information. Sadly, it can be all too easy to know there are things that are fucked, but remain suspended in those shadowy feelings of guilt, shame, victimhood, or "not enoughness." In many cases that's because a shadowy issue has been seen without the integration, and again, doing this work without integration will just leave you digging up demons. And if you have a victimhood shadow that gluttons on the kind of shame that absolves any personal responsibility, this is exactly the most delicious place to be.

Since shadow work is truly an illumination process, you can get a lot of powerful information from exploring the details of these shadows. This can help you get the clarity that will help you reach the stage of integration where you are more empowered, conscious of your choices, and free from self-sabotage and lack. Again, since this is inherently deep and serious work, there's a lot of value to approaching this work in a more fun and lighthearted way, like crafting a shadow cast of characters that represent your shadows.

To craft your own shadow personas, a few points need to be recognized. First, you must understand that every shadow fills a need. There is always a purpose or method to the madness that they wreak. If there was truly no benefit, be it avoidance, attention, self-preservation, or *some* way that it is serving you (even if it seems outright insane to insinuate such a thing), then they would extinguish on their own. In the shadow realm, there is a lot of misguided protective shit or maladaptive primal impulse that speaks to your most base urges. This is one of the first hard-to-accept aspects of working with the shadow. However, you are not going to get anywhere in lasting terms (meaning integration) unless you can make note of not only how badly these shadows are fucking with you, but also how they are *serving* you so you can address those needs elsewhere.

Next, understand that your catalog of shadows took root somewhere, somehow. This means that for every shadow, triggered response, fear, or sinister impulse there is an associated rich history of how you developed and incorporated this shadow into the folds of your subconscious. While it's easier for some shadows than others to pinpoint their origin story and lore, they all have some sort of history that is important to acknowledge. This may take some time.

Talk It Out

Sit somewhere comfortably and imagine a shadow persona like the inner critic is right there in front of you. Explore how this persona got there, how it feels about its role, and what purpose it is serving.

Talk with your shadow:

1. Begin speaking aloud to it, letting whatever wants to come out come out.

2. Afterward, write about the experience. What do you say to your shadow persona? How does this feel?

_____

_____

_____

_____

Another thing to acknowledge is where these shadows feel present in the body. For instance, a confidence shadow may feel like a sharp inward breath, a heaviness in the chest, or a feeling of swelling in the head and behind the eyes when you are "seen." An abandonment shadow may feel like a stone in your belly, or like your center of gravity is sinking into your feet.

Further considerations: How old does this shadow feel? Is this shadow reflecting a feeling in you of childlike incompetence? Does it feel like an exhausted four-hundred-year-old creature that's beyond sick of everyone's shit? Is your inner critic a crotchety old lady? All of these are creative compositions, but you can get some truly interesting info by leaning into these questions.

Write It Out

The following prompt can help steer your exploration of how your shadows came to be and help you flesh them out into full, three-dimensional personas.

Answer the following prompts to explore your shadows:

One of my strongest, most present shadows is:

_____

This shadow feels about _____ years old.

This shadow's personality is:

_____

_____

_____

Feelings and emotions that are associated with this shadow include:

_____

_____

_____

_____

I feel the presence of this shadow in my life in the following ways:

_____

_____

_____

_____

The associated history and personal myth and lore that is associated with this shadow includes:

_____

_____

_____

_____

This shadow has protected and benefited me in the following ways:

_____

_____

_____

_____

This shadow has limited and held me back in the following ways:

_____

_____

_____

_____

After identifying your cast of shadow characters, you may want to meditate on them, draw or paint them, continue talking to them, work with them through cards or other symbolic or divination tools (if that's your thing), or engage with them in some other way. This can be an ongoing process.

Integration Tip

Discovering the multiple faces of the shadow is helpful for integration as it can help us get a sense of which shadows may be acting up and which needs they may be serving. There may be different strategies we use to illuminate and integrate each depending on the specific ways they're experienced and expressed, so keep in touch with what feels right and helpful for you.

Chapter 15

Triggers and Sore Spots
Feeling Your Core Wounds

When we begin to see our shadows' presence in our lives, we can learn more by viewing them through the lens of our triggers and core wounds. Every trigger is an invitation for shadow work: We are being given behavioral and emotional "bread crumbs" that can lead us to our innermost wounds.

Some definitions for the purposes of this chapter:

- **Trigger:** An activation—an immediate object or event that flares a noticeable and powerful emotional reaction as it hits the tender, exposed nerve of a preexisting core wound.

- **Core Wound:** The deeper insecurity, pain, vulnerability, or negative belief that causes distress and can poison the well of our worldview, tainting how we feel about both ourselves and the world.

Although the word "trigger" is thrown around a lot in a variety of contexts in popular culture, this chapter explores how and why these matter in the context of shadow work. We can regain control of our emotional worlds in a big way once we gain a really solid understanding of our triggers and how they interact with our internal core wounds.

Core wounds operate as the background programming of the shadow realm itself. In many cases, these core wounds inform how your shadows develop, how they are expressed, how they are felt, and certainly how they are triggered. To put it simply, although you are exposed to a variety of triggers throughout any given day, you only feel the sting of them if they hit the exposed nerve of a particular core wound.

For example: If someone has a core wound of abandonment, they may notice a situation where they are dismissed or rejected by a friend or lover and be sent into a spiral over it, whereas someone who does not have this core wound may not even notice or interpret the situation in such a way at all. If a person has a core wound of insecurity and "not enoughness," they may find it incredibly painful to receive even minor criticism at work, whereas someone who does not have such a core wound may take the critique in stride. Your menu of triggers will be solely unique to you, formed by your own particular experiences and the intensity of how these experiences impacted you and are recalled.

Write It Out

Can you identify some patterns in the things that are triggering for you? These can include the behavior of others, certain situations and scenarios, interactions with others, and how you feel about yourself.

_____

_____

_____

_____

_____

_____

_____

Your core wounds developed alongside you and are influenced and interpreted by your subjective awareness (whether conscious or unconscious). As such, they are as uniquely personal as your fingerprints or DNA. In many cases core wounds are developed in childhood, as you may have experienced deeply impactful or painful experiences like rejection, neglect, instability, trauma, and more. That being said, it's important to acknowledge that what happens in childhood isn't the only source of core wounds. They can arise at any point across the lifespan when something deeply impactful or traumatic happens. For example, a person can be fairly confident then make one bad decision as an adult that leads to lasting self-trust issues. Other core wounds can include:

- Shame

- Fear

- Control (craving too much of it or feeling a lack of it)

- Abandonment

Core wounds can be pervasive in how they are expressed throughout your life. In fact, particular responses to triggers can be widely varied even if multiple people have the same core wound. For instance, one person with a core wound of shame may react with anger when triggered, while another may respond by retreating within themselves.

These wounds can poison what you think of yourself. Typically, these wounds ultimately boil down to one larger wound, which is, "I am not good enough as I am." Instead, people often carry shadowy ideas of being wretched, villainous creatures, greasy little impostors that can carry a constant feeling of waiting for the other shoe to drop before they finally get found out for being just a collection of shitty personality traits in a trench coat.

In many cases, core wounds can get passed down to you and you learn them through modeling. When your caregivers operate from their own wounds when interacting with you, together you can become a dynamic system of exposed nerves bumping into one another causing pain and drama. You not only learn some of these generational or programmed wounds by the way you are treated by your care providers, but also by observing and learning from the things they causally do or say. For instance, a parent with a core wound of fear may speak of the world as an unkind place and communicate that it's better to stay safe and not break the mold in front of their child. Although they may not be consciously trying to pass on this fear-based limitation, they are showing their true beliefs through their words and actions. Another example would be that of shame. A parent with deep shame wounds or taboos around certain topics (more on this in Chapter 20) may unintentionally pass these beliefs on to their child through the verbal judgments they make about others and the way they show what is "acceptable" conduct.

You also can develop core wounds from the larger collective unconscious of humankind. This may include the cultural ideals of society (for example, beauty standards and the idea that people are always just a few products away from finally being acceptable).

In order to find your own core wounds, you must recognize your triggers as being symptoms of a deeper underlying dis-ease.

Fill It Out

The following prompt will walk you through tracing your triggers back to the deeper core wounds they are caused by. To begin, think of something that triggered you recently. Feel free to use this format whenever you are triggered to uncover the root wound of each trigger.

Trigger: _____

_____

When I was triggered by this situation, it brought up feelings like:

_____

_____

When I was triggered, I felt _____ in my body.

Other memories I have associated with this feeling include:

_____

_____

_____

_____

I usually try and numb or cope with these feelings in the following ways:

_____

_____

_____

_____

The belief that these triggers expose is _____

_____,

leading me to think the core wound is one of _____

_____.

The earliest memory I have associated with this core wound in my life is:

_____

_____

_____

_____

Upon reflection, I've discovered that this core wound manifests in my life in the following ways that may have felt unrelated in the past:

_____

_____

_____

_____

Now that I am aware of this core wound, I'd like to ask what it is trying to do for me. My thoughts on this question:

_____

_____

_____

_____

I can take control of filling that need in a more empowered way by:

_____

_____

_____

_____

⧜ Integration Tip

Whenever you feel triggered, you can see this as a learning opportunity. It takes some time and effort, but by exploring these events, you can learn a lot about yourself. Once you walk back this process of finding your core wounds through your triggers, you can allow yourself to bounce back more quickly in the future when these circumstances pop up again.

Chapter 16

Your Authentic Self
Showing Up for You

Although living a life that's authentic and free seems like it should be the easiest way to move through life, the reality is that it's incredibly challenging for us to break through the bullshit and feel empowered to be who we truly are boldly, loudly, and publicly.

To live a life of authenticity is to first and foremost be truly okay with who you are, making your own unique self-expression your preferred comfort zone. This requires an understanding that your authentic and true nature is lovable, acceptable, and has the right to exist without reservations. No requirements to be perfect, no pressure to always get it "right." You are worthy and capable of just being, and you must back this up among your own council of demons before being able to energetically back yourself in the face of judgments from the outside world.

Stepping into your authenticity will always expose and trigger your shadows, because when you step into your power and express who you *truly* are (the good, the bad, *and* the ugly), you essentially drop all of the programming and allow yourself to just *be*....You are in essence enacting a subliminal "I am good enough as I am," an action you take only for *you*, and not for pleasing others.

Think It Out

Reflecting on the way you currently engage in your life, how safe, free, and confident are you in being fully authentic? Feel into your body as you reflect: Does the topic of whether or not you are standing firm in your authenticity feel activating for you? Where do you feel it?

Write out your reflections:

_____

_____

_____

_____

_____

_____

Many of us have had multiple shadow-building experiences that have shaped the way we relate to our authenticity. As a social species, we carry a deep desire to belong and be accepted by the group. An interesting side effect of this is a subconscious slip into conformity—after all, most of us have seen and experienced situations where we (or someone else) allowed ourselves to embrace our authenticity and been met with ridicule, scorn, anger, jealousy, and a whole host of other weird fucky energy.

Sadly, it can be more tempting to try to avoid triggering those negative reactions from others than to make the effort to avoid perpetual self-betrayal.

The important thing to understand is that everyone is in this boat together and the fear of unleashing your authenticity is one that is generational, societal, and shared. This is where you get to see the interplay of shadow as it propagates interpersonally and through the collective. As you learned in the previous chapter, your caregivers have a big influence on the development of your shadows. In fact, seeing authentic expression can be a trigger for their own shadowy wounds, and they may have reacted by discouraging this authenticity in you while you were growing up. It is important to recognize that it is rarely a conscious decision to propagate these ideas, but more a programmed response that ends up becoming both a societal and generational wound. This is why it's important to not only suspend self-judgment in shadow work, but understand how you were treated throughout your life in the spirit of non-judgment toward others.

If you want to do your part to break the cycle, you must commit to yourself and back yourself up wholeheartedly.

Write It Out

Let's take a moment to explore your thoughts and feelings toward embracing your authenticity:

I feel embarrassment, fear, or shame in stepping into my power as my authentic self because:

_____

_____

_____

_____

I first remember feeling this way in relation to being authentic when:

_____

_____

_____

_____

Now, you may be reading this feeling confused as fuck because your authentic self might feel a million miles away. Although you explored your stripped-down, authentic version of yourself in Phase 1 of this book, the reality is that who you authentically are is a relationship that must be maintained over time. You must connect to who you truly are on a rolling, ongoing basis. People are always in a state of evolution, even if it may not feel like it. When you fall into autopilot to keeping up a performance of who you think you are, you lose touch with yourself in the moment.

It is a great privilege of the deprogramming and self-acceptance process to not only uncover who you are, but to also integrate this information as part of your self-acceptance, expression, and understanding. I assure you, the joy and freedom that will come from getting to know that person is well worth the struggle to dig for them.

Real talk: Nobody has who they authentically are on lock 100 percent of the time. You are constantly growing, shifting, changing, and evolving, which means that who you are and how you outwardly express that is also constantly in a state of flux. When you approach the authenticity conversation, it's important to realize that part of unveiling authenticity is sometimes readjusting who you are. Over the lifespan, your values and needs and desires will shift, which can lead to shifts in even your deepest understanding of who you are. Being authentic in many cases is simply a willingness to approach yourself with curiosity and a desire to learn who you might be in that very given moment. So if you feel as if your authenticity is alien to you, you are really not that far behind anyone else who is doing the messy work of getting to know themselves and making adjustments in real time.

You are always in exactly the right place, and a return to self is not a return to past versions of you; it is simply a reconnection to who you are in any given moment.

So whether your authentic self feels like lost change in the couch or a brand-new element, taking up the cause of finding, loving, and connecting with it is always gonna be worthwhile. Give yourself permission to play and show up for *you*.

Write It Out

In the beginning of this book you made a commitment to yourself. This is also a good tool to keep you on track at any stage of the shadow work game. Let's pause for a moment and make another commitment to self—this time as your pre-integration prep work for letting your authenticity shine.

Read and initial each statement, customizing as necessary, making a promise and commitment to yourself:

_____   I am ready to begin building capacity to step into my power as my authentic self.

_____   I understand that this may be uncomfortable at first, but I am committed to persisting until the discomfort fades.

My motivation for unleashing my authentic self is:

_____

_____

_____

My shadowy resistance to unleashing my authentic self comes from:

_____

_____

_____

_____   In the spirit of love and acceptance, I release my shadowy resistance to claiming my authenticity with gratitude.

I will begin by taking the following simple actionable steps to practice:

_____

_____

_____

When I am met with situations that trigger my shadows, I will recalibrate through the following methods:

_____

_____

_____

_____ I give myself permission to tackle this goal in the spirit of love.

_____

[Sign Here]

〜 Integration Tip

Visualization can help you build capacity in a safe way, helping your brain to "practice" experiencing situations before they occur. Visualize what it would look like, and more importantly feel like, to allow yourself to step into your authenticity. The first barrier in any confidence or authenticity work is to get past the first gatekeeper: yourself! Once this is mastered, it is easier to get past any objections or weird energy from the outside, as you will have practiced energetically backing yourself. Let your visualization act as your motivation to stick with it as you move into Phase 3 of your shadow work, and push past any discomfort.

Chapter 17

Trapped Feelings!
Feeling Yourself with a Body Map

Being a human being can be mentally exhausting. Every moment of every day you seem to run an emotional and energetic gauntlet. The overthinking! The decision-making! The multiple attempts to thrive despite the baggage you carry! Unfortunately, this can cause you to numb out the primal sensations of your body, which in turn can hold you back when it comes to healing.

Your shadows may be fractured elements of you on a personality level, but the truth of the matter is that you encounter and experience them in your physical body. The repressed emotions, internal struggles, and all the bits of lingering grief, anger, insecurity, and emotions that you haven't dared face—they can manifest in the body in downright spooky ways.

The mind-body connection is just what it sounds like: the interaction between the body and the mind! This flows in both directions, as the body can influence the mind, and the mind can have very real impacts on the body. All of this shit is uniquely and powerfully entwined in the greater ecosystem that is *you*!

The mysteries of the mind-body connection have been a hot topic of scientific inquiry for ages, with studies and discoveries happening constantly. The greater the understanding you can get on how this connection works, the better the results you will get not only when it comes to physical wellness, but also in the areas of mental wellness and working with your shadows.

Feel It Out

Explore your mind-body connection:

1. Lie down in a place where you are unlikely to be interrupted, and begin doing a "body interview" by turning your focus to each part of your body one at a time.

2. Note the physical sensations that come up, and whether there is an associated emotion(s) that may be present in each body part. As you focus on each body part, breathe deeply and acknowledge the feelings and shadows there, then exhale and relax that body part as much as you can. Do this from the top of your head to the tips of your toes.

3. Write out your thoughts after this exercise.

_____

_____

_____

_____

_____

_____

The first and simplest place for any person (like you!) to begin acknowledging the role of the body in shadow healing is to train yourself to identify how and where you feel activations in your body. Throughout this book, you've explored how to spot shadowy interference in your life, as well as investigated these shadows themselves in more depth. The next step is to connect these shadows to the body. How are they physically felt? And where?

Draw It Out

Reflect on how your physical sensations align with your shadows by making yourself a body map! To do this, make a list of emotions you feel and assign a color to each one. Then draw an outline of your body. Start marking each part of your body with the sensations you observed in the first prompt in this chapter. Once these are marked, consider what emotions from your list may be tied to those sensations. Color in the parts of your body map accordingly. In some cases, you may feel certain sensations and correlated emotions in more than one area, or you may process multiple different emotions in one body part. However it comes together for you is exactly how it should be. The important part is to build this awareness of how and where your body feels things so you can help yourself process your emotions more fully.

Draw your body map here:

An important part of the investigation phase of shadow work is to learn how and where you feel activations within the body. As with the rest of the shadow realm, this will be wholly unique to *you*. Some people are generally just more tapped into their bodies when it comes to feeling into or pinpointing emotion, while others feel clueless when it comes to this. However, this is a skill of somatic observational awareness that can be cultivated in *anyone*. Like tying your shoes, it's something that can be practiced. We've peeked at the topic of somatic awareness in earlier chapters, for example when talking about triggers, but the topic deserves a more thorough look.

Fill It Out

To continue exploring the common shadowy triggers and activations in your physical body, use the following Fill It Out prompt as a journaling companion to your body map. You may feel some of these in multiple areas of your body. If you are unsure, try to bring your awareness to your body the next time you experience these feelings, and come back to this prompt.

Fill in the blanks to further explore your triggers and body map:

When I feel unsafe, I feel it in my_____.

When I feel fearful, I experience it in my _____.

When I am "numbing out," I feel it in my _____.

When I feel excited, I feel it in my_____.

When I am experiencing my intuition, I feel it in my_____.

When I experience shame, I feel it in my _____.

When I feel hopeful, I feel it in my_____.

When I feel angry, I feel it in my _____.

§ **Integration Tip**
Numbing out is a way we can further repress our shadowy feelings, but in a somatic way. When we allow ourselves to process the mental and emotional fuckery we are going through by tapping in and fully experiencing it in the physical body, we actually become more capable of quickly and effectively moving through the feelings. This is how we can use somatic awareness to integrate and move through these feelings using the body.

In many cases, when shadows rise up, you can experience intense physical responses from your nervous system. This is sometimes described as the "acute stress response," but it mainly lives in the collective awareness as the "fight-flight-freeze-or-fawn" response. (Physiologist Walter Bradford Cannon coined the phrase "fight or flight"; it has been updated over the years to include the "freeze" and "fawn" responses.) Let's look at how these responses may lead to behaviors that help you minimize feeling what you are feeling in your body:

- **The Fight Response:** Aggressive outbursts that can act as a "release valve" (e.g., punching a hole in a wall so the emotional discomfort becomes physical pain).

- **The Flight Response:** Avoidance behaviors to minimize fear and anxiety in the body, such as avoiding intimacy with others or excessive exercise to avoid processing feelings.

- **The Freeze Response:** "Numbing out" behaviors, such as falling into mindless scrolling or dissociating from your body.

- **The Fawn Response:** Acquiescing to others with incessant praise, etc., to minimize the likelihood of feeling physically alarmed or unsafe in an interaction.

Consider how these responses from the nervous system have come up for you in the past when experiencing the emotions from the previous Fill It Out prompt.

Write It Out

Use this space or a separate journal to explore your past experiences with the different responses of the nervous system:

_____

_____

_____

_____

_____

_____

_____

_____

_____

_____

_____

_____

_____

_____

_____

_____

If you want to approach shadow work in a holistic way, it is very important that you do so factoring in the role of the body! It is very difficult to actually do the work necessary to address your shadows in an ongoing way if you don't.

Chapter 18

Prove It
Debunking Bodies of Evidence

We are always interfacing with the outside world through the lens of our mindset, worldview, and subjective experience. These can act as "filters" that determine the things that do and do not get through to our conscious awareness, the significance and impact they hold, and how they are interpreted (often through the lens of our desires or core wounds). When it comes to "objective reality," we are ill-equipped to experience whatever that would be without our own bullshit.

⚡ Integration Tip

Confirmation bias is an important thing to be aware of when it comes to shadow integration. This is the brain's tendency to seek out information and evidence that fits its preexisting beliefs. Although it may seem counterintuitive that you would bend your awareness to favor information that may support negative or painful subconscious beliefs, the hard truth is that doing so can help you feel like life is safe and predictable. Being aware of this tendency can help you reframe your understanding of yourself.

When you are operating with background beliefs and core wounds that are poisoning your perception and interpretation of life on an ongoing basis, you can wind up in a perpetual state of evidence-gathering or seeking out information that supports negative beliefs and experiences about life (and your place within it).

Write It Out

Before we get into the nitty-gritty of examining our beliefs, let's revisit some of the specifics of what they actually are (similar to the work we did in Phase 1). Working through some of these in more depth will allow us to lay the groundwork for putting these beliefs to the test.

Answer the following questions to further explore your beliefs:

1. What kind of mindset and worldview do you have about yourself?

_____

_____

_____

_____

- Can you think of when these beliefs originated?

_____

_____

_____

_____

2. What kind of mindset and worldview do you have about others?

_____

_____

_____

_____

- Can you think of how these beliefs came to be?

_____

_____

_____

_____

3. What kind of mindset and worldview do you have about the world in general?

_____

_____

_____

_____

- Is this a mindset you feel you want to have about the world, or has it just happened subconsciously along the way?

_____

_____

_____

_____

In Phase 1, you explored the concept of patterns, beliefs, and biases that manifest in your life on behalf of your shadows. Now you are tasked with critically examining those patterns, biases, and beliefs, and the evidence you've gathered to support them. Is any of that even true? What proof do you have?

In any mindset work I do with people, I begin with introducing the concept of what I call "bodies of evidence": that big ol' pile of experiences, circumstances, and occurrences that feeds your shadowy beliefs about yourself, the world, and what's possible for you. For example:

- Every person who believes you cannot experience love without pain likely has a body of experiential evidence to support this belief.

- Every person who believes that letting other people close will result in getting fucked over likely has a body of experiential evidence to support this belief.

- Every person who believes that anything they try will be destined to fail or leave them worse off than when they started will likely have a body of experiential evidence to support this belief.

However, when you take a cup of life experience and stir in a pinch of cognitive bias, what you're left with isn't reality at all. It's a recipe for stewing in your shadows. For every body of evidence you have compiled to support the beliefs that limit and restrict you, there is likely another hidden body of evidence that supports an alternative view. It is your preexisting shadowy belief systems and differential attribution of importance to these events through confirmation bias that paint a picture that *this is your reality and always will be.*

To revisit the previous examples:

- Every person who believes you cannot experience love without pain likely has a body of experiential evidence where they may have been loved deeply, even if they were not aware of it.

- Every person who believes that letting other people get close to them will result in getting fucked over likely has a body of experiential evidence where other people were safe, generous, and kind.

- Every person who believes that anything they try will be destined to fail or leave them worse off than when they started will likely have a body of experiential evidence where this was not the case, or they may have built this up internally because the fear itself may have moved them to inaction.

This isn't to invalidate your experience at all, but simply a call to gently reexamine it.

Unfortunately these programs run deep, so it involves some work to access or collect alternative evidence in your awareness. In many cases, shitty shadowy attitudes can gatekeep more supportive experiences (or opportunities or relationships) from entering into your awareness through the patterns and cycles of misery they keep you in. You essentially give differential weights to these experiences based on *what you already believe to be true.*

Write It Out

Returning to the prompt earlier in this chapter, make a couple of lists for each point of your bodies of evidence. The experiences, circumstances, and interactions that supported each point, *and* the experiences, circumstances, and interactions that provide conflicting evidence that those beliefs may not be objectively true.

Explore your beliefs with evidence in the following prompts:

1. Mindset and worldview you have about yourself:

_____

_____

- Evidence to support this belief:

_____

_____

_____

_____

- Evidence to conflict this belief:

_____

_____

_____

_____

2. Mindset and worldview you have about others:

_____

_____

- Evidence to support this belief:

_____

_____

_____

_____

- Evidence to conflict this belief:

_____

_____

_____

_____

3. Mindset and worldview you have about the world in general:

_____

_____

- Evidence to support this belief:

_____

_____

_____

_____

- Evidence to conflict this belief:

_____

_____

_____

_____

It is very important, not only in the context of shadow work but as you move through life in general, to be open to constantly reexamining your mindset, worldview, and belief systems. Make sure that you are consciously experiencing life, and not just interpreting the world through the lens of your wounds.

People often take these beliefs and this "evidence" a step further, using them to make inferences about the future and what is available for them. However, this is also flawed. Just because XYZ thing happened in the past does not make it an accurate representation of what is going to happen in the future. To believe it so is to keep yourself stuck and in a cycle of noticing and experiencing the same patterns over and over in agonizing perpetuity.

Your future is truly an open road of opportunity, limited only by your ability to navigate the direction in which you are headed. Well, that and the blind, unpredictable winds of circumstance! So no more future-forecasting through the wounds of the past. Deal?

Fill It Out

Clarity and intention are a key part of shadow work, so with the following prompt you will practice opening up your mindset. You can investigate both your current beliefs and the beliefs you desire to have.

Read, fill in the blank, and initial each statement, customizing as necessary, making a promise and commitment to yourself:

____ I am open to a future that is _____

_____.

____ I am open to collecting evidence that_____

_____.

____ I am open to honing my awareness to see _____

_____.

____ I am committed to cultivating a mindset that is _____

_____.

____ I am ready to release past pains and open up to new ways of experiencing the world around me.

_____

[Sign Here]

Chapter 19

Worthiness Unmasked
Deconstructing the Things You Did and Didn't "Deserve"

There are a lot of behaviors, circumstances, and beliefs that we can find within the hidden corners of our shadows that fundamentally come down to harboring feelings that we are *fundamentally not good enough*.

Some examples:

- A person who feels deeply unworthy of the things they have may engage in self-sabotaging behavior in order to lose them.

- A person who struggles with feeling unworthy may adjust who they are to be accepted by others.

- Angry outbursts and controlling behavior is sometimes a power mask for those who have deep worthiness wounds.

- People with worthiness wounds may struggle to improve their lives or circumstances because they do not believe deep down that they are worthy of better things.

Feeling unworthy is sadly a very relatable issue. Many (if not most) people struggle with some level of worthiness hang-ups. And it can manifest in different ways in different people and across the lifespan.

But let's take a minute to brush off the casual relatability of the topic and really sit with this: *Unworthiness is a feeling that you are fundamentally not good enough*. This feeling can be so incredibly painful, and the impact of feeling it on an ongoing basis cannot be understated. Running with this concept as a part of your background operating system will drain your energy, zap your self-esteem, collar your potential and creativity, and leech out in ways that are incomprehensible in scale. Unworthiness wounds can be a steady source of toxicity in your worldview and self-concept, and it is absolutely fundamental that you face these wounds in order to have the best experience of life possible.

Write It Out

Write about the theme of worthiness. How do you feel this theme has played out in your life so far? Get as specific as you can:

_____

_____

_____

_____

_____

_____

_____

_____

_____

_____

_____

If you struggle with feelings of low worthiness (or even the other extreme—an *inflated* sense of worthiness, which is typically a mask for some other more vulnerable emotion), the well is poisoned. But great news, my dude: This, like any other mental trap, is totally fixable!

⩰ Integration Tip

Anytime you find yourself being caught up in a worthiness trap it can be helpful to zoom out and conceptualize the role of worthiness in nature. Do fish, or trees, or flowers feel the need to be worthy? Is this simply an agonizing artifact of being a prosocial, conscious species? Ask yourself this: Do you feel like others must earn their worthiness, or is this a special kind of gauntlet you save for yourself?

Holding an idea of whether or not you "deserved" the things that have happened to you can be fertile ground for some truly somber shadows to take root. Sadly, these ideas often form in very early developmental stages, becoming part of the personal narratives that people use to define themselves and interpret the "bodies of evidence" they collect throughout life.

I want to be crystal fucking clear when I say that there is no benefit to viewing your life or the world in these terms. Although it feels logical, it's not. Although it feels justified, it isn't.

The messy reality is that sometimes *shit just happens*. There is rarely ever any rhyme or reason to what happens and why. Bad things happen to good people, good things happen to bad people, and everything in between. A large element of existence is luck of the draw—pure undirected circumstance, random rolls of the dice in the chaotic soup of life. No child deserves to be born into war or famine, and yet it happens. Many people deserve more (or less) than what they get. The idea of justice is a fundamentally human way of trying to make sense of the drama of existence. But on the most fundamental level, many debts go unpaid and worthiness has absolutely fucking nothing to do with any of it.

Write It Out

Answer the following questions to dig deeper, and explore your thoughts about worthiness:

1. What are your ideas and beliefs about justice and what people do and don't deserve?

_____

_____

_____

_____

2. Do you find unfairness to be a trigger of your own shadowy feelings?

    ○ Yes   ○ No

If yes, explore that trigger:

_____

_____

_____

_____

To be clear, having a sense of justice is not a *bad* thing. As a pro-social species, we have evolved to think this way for the benefit of the group. It's when we weaponize these ideas against ourselves in order to prop up shadows of shame and unworthiness that we leave ourselves at risk of falling into traps of learned helplessness and the feeling of being "stuck." We end up doing mental gymnastics to buy into the idea that it's somehow our fault. Similarly, it's this attachment to justice and fairness that can leave us waiting for years on closure that will never come, or postponing our healing to wait for other people to either participate or "get theirs." This is a shadowy trap of epic proportions!

Shadow work is full of hard truths, and one hard truth is this: Holding on too tight to ideas of justice and fairness can sometimes leave you contributing to your own struggle in a big way. Only *you* are responsible for your healing and forward motion, and the only justice you are entitled to is that which you can give yourself. Anything beyond this is truly a bonus.

And in terms of worthiness, the hard truth is that you are responsible for recognizing *your own* self-worth. No amount of outside validation or affection can fill the gaping void that low self-worth can leave within. And often, the thing driving you to want to fill this void is the shadow. Low self-worth can lead people to try to find self-worth in pleasing others or getting praise on tap. It can lead to paralysis and self-sabotage. It takes courage and determination to begin crawling out of that hole, but when you do, you will be able to affirm yourself whenever you may need it, take responsibility, and find more and more of yourself along the way.

Write It Out

Explore the following questions about hard truths and wounds you may be harboring:

1. When it comes to self-worth and personal responsibility, are there any hard truths you feel you need to face about the wounds you may be harboring?

_____

_____

_____

_____

2. Can you thank these wounds for serving you in some way?

　　　○　Yes　　　　　　　○　No

If yes, express that feeling here, and explore ways in which these wounds are serving you:

_____

_____

_____

_____

_____

_____

In some cases, these worthiness wounds may take some time, hard fucking work, and possibly therapy to heal. In other cases, you may be able to flip the script on your own with just some focused effort. There is no one-size-fits-all approach, but I promise you that no matter what approach you take, healing worthiness wounds will always be an extremely beneficial use of your time, effort, and energy.

Remember: You do not need to *earn* your worth. You are worthy just as you are, and coming to understand this is first and foremost an *inside job.*

Chapter 20

Naughty Business
Exploring Your Taboos

Sometimes the shadow reveals itself when confronting things that feel extremely off-limits. Topics like sex, politics, finances, and the like can flare us up in big ways because of their taboo nature, and just like a child when told not to say swear words, the naughty nature of these taboo things can make them wield even more power over us.

Write It Out

Answer the following prompts to explore some of your taboos:

1. What are some things that are taboo or off-limits for you?

_____

_____

_____

_____

_____

2. How did they come to have this status?

_____

_____

_____

_____

_____

3. Were you told that they were, or did you develop these ideas yourself along the way?

_____

_____

_____

_____

_____

Perhaps in your experience, talking about these things was considered uncomfortable, impolite, or simply not tolerated. You may have even gotten such a big hairy response out of others that it taught you a lesson for life about the dangers of addressing *The Big Taboo Thing.* Can you think of anything more shadowy than that? Essentially the shadows are the things that get stuffed into the basement of the psyche because they feel difficult or uncomfortable to face, or because you learned that doing so wasn't in your best interest. In the case of wider cultural taboos, you can see how the repression of addressing or talking about these things on a collective scale can only lead to more repression, trauma, and bullshit going forward.

An absolute and unavoidable fact is this: That which you are afraid to face is that which will continue festering unseen. This is nonnegotiable, and everyone suffers for it.

Write It Out

Think of something that feels taboo or off-limits for you, and reflect on the following questions:

1. What is your aversion to talking about it? What could happen?

_____

_____

_____

_____

_____

_____

2. What has happened historically in your experience or in your family of origin when talking about it?

_____

_____

_____

_____

_____

_____

3. What feelings rise up for you as a result of facing this off-limits thing?

_____

_____

_____

_____

_____

_____

Shadow work at its core is about digging in the darkness to find the light. The reason why this work is not approached casually by the masses is because doing it can be very bleak indeed. Specifically in the case of taboos, there can be some downright terrifying demons to be met that can leave people feeling ungrounded and unsafe (for good reason). Things that are taboo for you are sometimes a reflection of your personal trauma or ideals, but more often, these are things that also reflect the collective shadow. And when it comes to taboos, the collective shadow can end up having a ripple effect that reverberates through generations. Some examples:

- Sexual abuse and trauma

- Poverty and the traumas that come with it

- Inequity, abuses, and marginalization

- Mental health issues and stigmatization

- And many, many more

Sexuality is a great example of a taboo that has wide and far-reaching implications across both the personal and collective shadow. Most people live in a culture that's been influenced by purity ideals. While this is getting significantly better in recent years, the topic of sex is still considered somewhat taboo, even though it is a perfectly normal dimension of the human experience (and healthily so, provided every-thing is consensual and there's a level playing field when it comes to power dynamics). The implication of this cultural collective aversion to speaking freely about sex is that many people repress aspects of their own sexuality, associate it with deep feelings of shame, or avoid the topic altogether. Not only can they feel insecure about their own sexual nature, but they may also be passing on this shame and avoidance to the next generation. The statistics on the prevalence of sexual abuse paint a jarring picture of how treating sex as a taboo has impacted the world—and one that isn't even a full picture due to underreporting. Because of the taboo nature of the topic and the associated feelings of shame, many victims of sexual abuse are afraid to come forward and make waves. The culture of silence is beginning to break down, but there is still a lot of fucking work that needs to be done.

Now, this example of a taboo is huge and there are so many ways in which it intersects with the shadow. So if this is something that has influenced your life, please first understand that you are not alone, and if you are able to access the trained guidance of a professional, please do so. Your life and happiness are important, and you deserve gentle and loving space to heal.

In many cases, from sex to money, our taboos are rooted in feelings of shame. If we dared break the taboo of speaking about these things, this relationship was likely reinforced by those around us and we were left with shameful feelings. It's been said many times throughout this workbook, but it bears repeating: We cannot fight repression with repression. We take our power back by healing our relationship to shame, and confronting the legitimacy of a taboo topic and understanding why it has been put "off-limits." Take a stand to talk about taboo topics, to help drag them out into the light.

Even if the example of sex doesn't apply to your experience, there's a good chance that you do have an aversion toward certain taboo topics and that this avoidance and repression is affecting your life in some way. As a part of your shadow work efforts, it's important to critically examine what these repressive feelings are and where they came from. Much like other elements of your worldview and belief systems, some of this shit just isn't legitimate and valid when you remove the aspect of cultural and family conditioning.

Personal taboos can form the basis of what holds people back in life, and influences the energy they bring to the world. For example, if you see talking about mental health issues as taboo and you're a parent, you may be raising your kids to have this as a taboo as well; this may hold them back from seeking help if they do have a mental health struggle of their own. Particularly when it comes to shame, avoiding the taboo maintains the choke hold that feeling has over the world, which can lead down a stormy path of self-destruction. Frankly, you deserve better!

Investigating your taboos with the goal to heal your relationship to them helps lift the shadow of the collective. It is meaningful, powerful work.

Write It Out

The following prompt is meant to help you investigate your taboos with an emphasis on empowering yourself to take that understanding and clarify what a healed relationship with these taboos would look like.

Fill in the blanks and answer the prompts to further investigate your taboo topics:

I am going to bring healing to the taboo topic of _____

_____.

The taboo nature of this topic has affected my life in the following ways:

_____

_____

_____

_____

_____

My motivation for addressing and healing the taboo nature of this topic in my awareness is:

_____

_____

_____

_____

_____

I believe that having a healthy and open relationship with this topic would look like this:

_____

_____

_____

_____

_____

Chapter 21

The Claws Go Deep
When Your Shadow Doesn't Want to Be Revealed

To engage in a loving relationship with your shadow can feel like a monumental challenge. It can be gut-wrenching to illuminate your shadow and recognize all the ways it may have been holding you back, putting you in shitty situations, and inciting you to bad behavior through the years. Being able to face the fact that maybe you were an unwilling participant in your own struggle isn't the easiest thing. Nor is being able to face the fact that maybe you've been the worst kind of bully to yourself or others, or facing the amount of personal responsibility you have over your own life experience and healing.

The truth is many people pick up shadow work, sometimes multiple times, and then promptly put it down again because it feels *just too damn heavy*. Sometimes a person just isn't ready, and that's okay. Better to do this work when you are stable and feel ready. But sometimes, even when you are ready, your ego doesn't want the shadow to be revealed.

On the whole, it's a lot easier on the ego to face the shadows that position you at a disadvantage. These include things like insecurity, people-pleasing, and inner child wounds. In these circumstances, you're positioned as the unwilling victim. And the best part is that in doing this work, you are also positioned as the virtuous hero that gets to bring you back to yourself. Sometimes, even that kind of powerful healing can be feeding into shadowy desires for control or martyrdom; it's a tricky thing to navigate, and once you start poking around in your own shadows, the learning never stops!

The hard truth is that shadow work is meant to be full of...well, *hard truths*! If your shadow work only feels completely freeing, vindicating, and triumphant, then you may not be digging hard enough.

Fill It Out

Let's look at a few hard truths that you've discovered through shadow work, either with this workbook or outside of it, and how far you may have gotten with exploring these things.

Fill in the blanks and answer the prompts to explore how far you've come:

Through my shadow work, I have encountered a hard truth, which is:

_____

_____

_____

When I made this realization, I felt _____ because

_____

_____.

On a scale of 0 to 5, 0 being not ready at all, and 5 being enthusiastically ready, I felt a readiness to handle being faced with this particular shadow of:

○ 1———○ 2———○ 3———○ 4———○ 5

I allowed myself to confront this issue in the following ways:

_____

_____

_____

_____

I feel like I could go further to address this issue when I am ready in the following ways:

_____

_____

_____

_____

Again, this isn't to say that shadow work should be *overly* hard and heavy, but just to note that some of the most fulfilling shadows to integrate in Phase 3 will be the ones that might make you cringe and experience some cognitive dissonance. And that's okay!

Recall the contract you filled out in the beginning of this workbook: Facing this stuff is only worthwhile when you are able to find loving acceptance for what you uncover.

Visualize It

Sit or lie down and visualize communicating with your ego.
Imagine giving your loving support to step aside and trust yourself to take good care of whatever you may find in the shadow realms. When you have done this, write your thoughts about the visualization.

_____

_____

_____

_____

_____

_____

I am a firm believer in the power of self-healing, especially given the dire lack of access to resources that some people face. However, I'm also a firm believer in accessing professional resources if you're able to. When it comes to shadow work, some things are better handled with the loving support of a coach, therapist, counselor, shaman, or whatever form of guidance you vibe with that you are able to access. Don't be afraid or embarrassed to seek outside help if you feel it could be beneficial.

If you are going to dive into shadow work, it's really important to understand that even if you have gone back and forth with it for _years_, getting frustrated, overwhelmed, and insecure along the way, this was not time wasted. There is no time limit on doing the work. Healing is not a race: It is an approach that sees life as a series of invitations and opportunities to respond accordingly. Sometimes that looks like being gung ho about your growth, and sometimes that looks like honoring your needs by continuing to rot on the couch. All things have their place!

You can only do as much as you can, and bringing the same kind of shaming, repressive, judgmental energy to illuminating your shadows will only make it all harder and more convoluted to integrate in

Phase 3. Shadow work is not meant to be a structured process of taking inventory of how much you've been victimized, or how much your life has sucked, or how shitty you are at coping with life. It is meant to be an exercise in self-love and understanding. You are not required to be perfect. You are not required to have it all figured out. You are only required to be compassionate and honest with yourself, and honor your needs along the way. That's it.

So if you aren't in a space where you are capable or prepared to do the work? For fuck's sake, take a break! Trust your inner compass, and do not use the shadow work process as yet another space to victimize and re-traumatize yourself. Give yourself permission to revisit this shit later!

Write It Out

Write a list of shadows or situations in which you feel a lack of confidence about tackling right now, even if it's just temporarily:

_____

_____

_____

_____

_____

_____

_____

_____

_____

_____

_____

Now, give yourself written permission to take on these things later, or seek guidance and support to help you do so. Sign it.

_____

_____

_____

_____

_____

_____

_____
[Sign Here]

⧚ Integration Tip

Shadow work is an ongoing process of inquiry and development. Don't lose sight of the reasons why we take up this work in the first place: to transform chaos into clarity and step into our authentic selves (the good, the bad, and the ugly). Plenty of people go through their lives not giving a single hot fuck about the shadow or how it is impacting their lives. You are doing this work as a gift of love to yourself. Let it feel like it is by approaching _yourself_ with love, kindness, and curiosity.

Phase Three

INTEGRATION AND SYNTHESIS
Vibing with Your Whole Self

In the first two phases of shadow work we got to know the shifty ways it's been slinking around our lives, gaining some understanding of how and why it developed. Now is the part where we dance with those demons and invite them into the whole of who we are.

Although "shadow integration" may sound like a vague side quest in the game of life, it doesn't need to be shrouded in a mystical haze. It's quite simply the process of accepting your shadow into your conscious awareness. In order to do this, you will be using the following chapter prompts and tips to neutralize all the bullshit that keeps you in the swamp of shame, judgment, or pressure to be a perfect and virtuous being who's got all your shit together. No one has it all figured out! Your shadows are to be accepted and integrated, *not* banished or tossed away.

Integration is without a doubt the most important part of shadow work. It is in integration that you breathe fully into the depths of your authenticity. As you will discover in the following pages, shadow integration can involve something as simple as recognizing your wounds and making efforts to be gentle with yourself, such as in your self-talk. It can also be found through setting yourself up for success with actionable plans that you stick to even after you've finished this workbook, such as a self-care plan. At all times shadow integration is about approaching yourself with compassion and resisting the urge to distance yourself from any aspects of who you are.

Although this is the phase where you explore integration more fully, you may have also noticed that integration tips are intentionally sprinkled throughout the other two phases to illustrate how it is an ongoing element of shadow work. Integration can happen quietly, or it can hit like a massive breakthrough. It can happen again and again, or at various points and times. It's all valid.

If you've ever seen those videos of the sun rising or setting over Stonehenge, you'll have an amazing visual of what shadow work is like. When the light is coming from one side of Stonehenge, the shadow moves to the other side. As the light passes around, the shadows lengthen, shorten, move, and essentially respond to the light. Your shadow work may be cyclical and dynamic just like this.

Chapter 22

Are You Feeling It?
Sitting with Your Shadow

A necessary part of understanding and integrating our shadows involves gaining the ability to sit with things that feel really fucking unpleasant without shutting down, numbing out, or turning away. Although it would be great if we all had monk-level powers of ego-transcending awareness, we are mostly just messy humans having a messy human experience, and sometimes rough feelings are just a part of that!

I truly believe that your life can only change in proportion to how much discomfort you're willing to allow yourself to feel. Nobody has ever climbed a mountain by being unwilling to get off the couch. Nobody has ever found fame while being avoidant to criticism. Nobody has ever truly engaged in shadow work if they're unwilling to hurt their own feelings. When it comes to shadow work (or pursuing any kind of disciplined or honest forward motion), you must have the ability to persist through feelings that objectively kind of suck.

One of the biggest barriers to lasting integration in shadow healing is resistance. Resistance is the response of your ego when facing things that you abso-fucking-lutely don't want to face. It's a totally normal, very human response to the messy uncomfortable business of shadow illumination. Think of it like an emotional cruise control: Anytime you are faced with something that challenges the carefully crafted idea of who you are, it sets off the alarm bells in your ego and resistance slips in to course-correct back to a place that feels safe and smooth. Resistance comes in endless forms; it can be blaming others or projecting, distracting yourself from facing hard things, outright denial, anger, and more. How and when it shows up can depend on the circumstances, but you can bet your sweet ass it *will* indeed show up along the way!

When it comes to integration, it is imperative that you learn how to sit with difficult truths without losing your cool, or falling back into a pattern of repressing the shit that gives you the icks. In practice, this is messy, inconvenient, and can feel emotionally and energetically destabilizing. However, it's a fundamental part of the process to navigate the felt experience of the shadow in order to truly integrate it and grow. Having the ability to maintain presence with the emotional sucker punches of shadow work is what will ultimately allow you to integrate them in a powerful way and reduce their control over you. This is what allows you to put space between your triggers and reactions, respond from your values instead of your programming, and build your capacity to do hard shit.

Like a muscle, your capacity to do this builds over time with practice and repetition, making the whole process easier and less painful in the long run.

Think It Out

Take some time when you're alone to practice simply "sitting with your shadow."

1. Sit cross-legged in a comfortable space, using your shadow work playlist or ritual you created in the beginning of this workbook to set a calm tone.

2. As if you were going to meditate, try clearing your mind of the mundane BS, but specifically focus on conceptualizing your shadow, including all the feelings associated with these parts of yourself. Let yourself simply feel these uncomfortable feelings without numbing out or mentally spiraling.

3. You can do this for as long as feels "right" for you, or you can set yourself a timer for about 15–20 minutes.

4. Write out your thoughts when you're done.

_____

_____

_____

_____

_____

_____

The discomfort you can feel from acknowledging and facing your shadows is totally human and normal; however, it's discomfort that only arises from a place of internal preprogrammed judgment. There is no real objective morality that comes into play beyond yourself. The reason you feel any discomfort at all with the expression of your shadows, whether it be guilt, shame, or surprise, is because of the resistance you feel when you recognize inconsistencies between your unconscious shadow and your ego (who you think you are) or your conscious values. This is why it is so fucking important to try your best to approach this whole conversation of the shadow with as little judgment as possible. This allows you to form a new frame of reference, and it lessens the burdensome emotional clusterfuck of doing this work.

There is truly nothing outside your own self-referential awareness that says any of the feelings, behaviors, or motivations you find in the shadow are objectively negative. It's all just relevant to culture, morals, and self-concepts. In order to build your capacity for observing hard truths, you have to get to a space where you can neutralize the emotional chaos by recognizing that value judgments are not objective facts. For example, if you saw your neighbor's dog pooping in their yard you would view it neutrally, but if you saw your human neighbor doing the same it would make you feel some type of way! The reality is that since both of them are mammals born on this planet, there is nothing objectively unusual about this behavior in either case (once you remove conditioning, values, and expectations).

Learning to view the shadow through the same kind of neutral filter will help your integration efforts.

Write It Out

Answer the following questions to explore feelings associated with your shadow:

1. What parts of your shadows make you the most uncomfortable and why?

_____

_____

_____

_____

_____

_____

2. What are the judgments you associate with each? Be as detailed and descriptive as possible.

_____

_____

_____

_____

_____

_____

Now revisit your answer to the previous question, removing the descriptive words and value judgments. Take what you're left with and make a neutralizing statement of acceptance. Because the reality is that we make these things more difficult to sit with when we judge them.

Ultimately your goal for integration is learning to increase your capacity for discomfort in a conscious way so that you don't get caught up in patterns of resistance and turning a blind eye to difficult truths. We cannot hear and learn from what we are actively running from or ignoring. The more unacceptable you tell yourself anything is, the less comfortable you'll be to sit with it without wanting to crawl out of your own skin. But don't worry, love, all the stories we were told in our younger years about facing the boogeyman head-on prepared you for this!

Although you may never get to a place where you fully neutralize the emotional toll of shadow work (you are only human after all), you'll be doing yourself a huge favor when you learn to sit with the discomfort that comes with facing hard truths and calling yourself out. Ultimately, this is the way you can take responsibility for lasting change, and work smarter not harder when it comes to shadow work.

Integration Tip

Viewing your shadow from a place of playful curiosity is an incredible hack for integration because it lets you reframe the discomfort that's a natural side effect of shadow illumination into something a little more accepting and judgment-free. For instance, when watching a toddler behave like a toddler, we give them grace. We roll our eyes, recognize that that's just what toddlers fucking do, and we move on, loving them regardless. In many cases the shadow can bring out our inner toddler, and that's okay! Roll your eyes, have a wee giggle at what a shit show it is to be a human, and move forward with love.

Chapter 23

Living with the Spooky Thing
Accepting Your Shadow

It's important to always keep in mind that shadow healing isn't a one-and-done thing. In fact, the "healing" in question is more of a process versus a destination, and shadow healing is more about learning to live with that spooky thing under the floorboards rather than banishing it entirely! Acceptance is the first step in truly integrating your shadow. Although we have talked a lot about acceptance thus far in this workbook, here is where we are going to explore the deeper work of actually gaining that acceptance.

Write It Out

If you were to hire a cleaner to come and clean your house, are you the type that would clean it first out of courtesy/embarrassment? A great prompt for really facing what you're resistant to accept is to ask yourself:

"If there was a way for someone else to come into my brain and poke around, what would I clean up first?" Reflect on this through writing:

_____

_____

_____

_____

_____

_____

_____

_____

_____

_____

_____

In many cases, a shadow is born from a lack of love and acceptance somewhere along the way. Your task in integrating and learning to live with your shadow is one of learning to love and accept those sullen and exiled bits of yourself that were ousted, tucked away, and dismissed! For this, you must empower yourself to recognize that you alone have the power to become whole again through suspending any judgy, shame-filled urges and witnessing your shadow as it *is*.

Simply notice, acknowledge, and even (gasp!) *accept* its presence.

As counterintuitive as it may sound, your shadow is actually nourished and given strength the more it is ignored, denied, and judged. Every time a shadow rears its ugly head and you respond in ways that do not vibe with your values and virtues, you have a choice to either move forward with compassion and curiosity or make a feast for demons! Indulging the urge to blame others, get sucked into a vortex of guilt and shame, or just bypass the experience altogether feeds into the bad energy rather than helping you be whole again. This denies you the opportunity to learn from whatever fuckery it is you are dealing with in the first place!

Write It Out

Explore the hard parts of your shadow with these questions:

1. What parts of your shadow that you are currently becoming aware of are you finding the most difficult to accept? Why?

_____

_____

_____

_____

_____

_____

As simple as it may sound, just a nonjudgmental acknowledgment of poor behavior or self-destructive urges can be the very first lil' baby step on a path to integration. Because again, integration isn't about striving for a path to purity. It's about recognizing that the human psyche is a full-spectrum clusterfuck of feelings, both heavy and free, dark and light! And all of these states are valid and necessary to make up the chaotic symphony of the human experience.

The aim is to peacefully coexist with your shadow, and as you may have experienced in life, it can be incredibly difficult to peacefully exist with that which you judge, blame, or attempt to ignore.

⚡ Integration Tip

Sometimes integration comes in the intentional moments we can put between our automatic and intentional responses. When facing a shadow, try taking a breath, and as you breathe, think, *How can I lovingly acknowledge my shadow here while also interrupting this pattern and choosing to respond differently?* You are on the path to ongoing acceptance and healing!

Write It Out

The next time you let your "lower self" take the wheel, instead of getting hung up in a space of denial ("It wasn't *my* fault!") or judgment ("OMG, I am the *worst* person *ever!*"), try giving yourself a loving statement of unconditional understanding and acceptance and see how that feels. Your statement can look something like this:

"Recently, I let my anger and frustration get the best of me and I behaved in a way that I am not proud of. I can recognize now that I felt so frustrated because it hit a deep core wound of not being understood. Even though I reacted in this way, I still love and accept myself and my shadow, and I commit to being even more compassionate to myself to help heal these wounds."

Craft your own statement of love and acceptance now, so you have it ready to go in situations where your shadow may pop up and fuck with your vibe:

Recently, I let my_____ get the best of me

and I _____.

I now recognize that I felt_____ because it hit a core

wound of _____.

Even though I _____,
I still love and accept myself and my shadow, and commit to being even more compassionate to myself to help heal these wounds.

A fundamental fact of existence is that sometimes multiple things can be true at the same time, and your ability and capacity to hold space for these tensions will help determine how much you struggle when it comes to navigating the tide.

You can cringe at your shadows and still make attempts to approach them with curiosity and love. You can recognize when you aren't giving your best behaviorally (to put it mildly), while extending yourself compassion and understanding. You can recognize the icky parts of your shadows, affirm that you aren't proud of them, and yet still initiate the process of having a healthy relationship with them.

Resistance and the urge to turn away is a natural part of the process. You cannot judge yourself for judging yourself! What's important is what you do with those urges. Do you fight repression with repression and continue to make the road harder, or do you get brutally honest with yourself and use that discomfort to catapult you into forward motion and healing?

My hope is that by this part of this workbook you are coming to understand the ways in which your shadow *is* inherently kinda lovable.

I mean, in many cases it developed to protect you, to process the things that you couldn't, and to help fulfill your needs (albeit in a misguided way). I like to conceptualize the shadow like an oddly high-maintenance but lovable pet. You rarely meet a person who complains about their anxious dog's seven-step bedtime routine or tendency to bark at the color blue. Typically, they are loved for who they are, even if they're acknowledged as a little neurotic!

Bring that same kind of love and unconditional acceptance to your shadows!

Chapter 24

Understanding to Action
Circuit-Breaking
Shadowy Behavior Patterns

Earlier in this workbook as part of the Phase 2 work, we talked about behavior as a form of communication (especially in Chapter 12), with four main functions. Building on this concept, we can use that understanding to approach the tricky task of *shifting* those behaviors by using something called the "ABC model." ABC stands for:

- **A:** Antecedent (what happens immediately before the target behavior)
- **B:** Behavior (the target behavior that occurs)
- **C:** Consequence (what happens immediately after the behavior)

In some cases in my previous work in inclusion, this model allowed me to suss out the function of the behavior that I was dealing with (by looking at the consequence) in order to try and meet that need before the behavior occurred. It also let me understand the triggers or contexts the behavior occurred in (the antecedents) so I could either avoid them, or better yet, work on creating coping strategies to minimize the likelihood of the behavior occurring.

I came to recognize that this model could be used in my own life as well to help me change pervasive behavior patterns. And as a personal development enthusiast and wellness witch, I recognized that it can be a transformative addition to any shadow work tool kit as well!

Here's an example of how this model can relate to the unique expression of the shadow:

A person who struggles with feelings of sexual insecurity and jealousy is out with their partner and they run into their partner's ex (the antecedent). This is triggering, and hits that insecurity shadow. This person then begins making passive-aggressive remarks (the shadowy behavior) to their partner, which elicits their partner to give them reassurance (the consequence).

This is just one example of the way that this framework could be used in relation to the shadow. If the person with insecurity was aware of this shadow, they could integrate that awareness and circuit-break this whole cycle by either admitting they were triggered and asking for reassurance in a direct way, or better yet, doing the confidence work that would neutralize the trigger.

Boom.

Write It Out

Consider a recent time you found yourself triggered and responding from your shadows. Can you use the ABC model to sort out what triggered you, which behavior it elicited, and what you may have gotten from it? You can use this process over and over again for addressing different circumstances that pop up.

The Situation:

_____

_____

_____

_____

- **A**ntecedent:

_____

_____

_____

_____

_____

- **B**ehavior:

_____

_____

_____

_____

_____

- **C**onsequence:

_____

_____

_____

_____

_____

Now, this process may not work for *all* shadows, but it can be helpful enough in addressing shadowy behavior patterns that it's worth exploring. This model is simple, easy to remember, and doesn't take a high level of introspection or self-awareness to be utilized. All you really need is to know the basics of *what actually happened* in a given situation. The self-awareness part enters the picture when you cut through the bullshit and get honest with yourself about what function the behavior might be filling. Again, this can be done in the spirit of curiosity and play. Although your shadows have been lovingly referred to as your demons throughout this workbook, you don't need to objectively demonize them. They're simply just unintegrated aspects of you coming out to play. It's your avoidance of them that makes them behave "poorly" (and by that I mean, in a way you may not understand or be proud of).

Write It Out

Let's take a moment to freewrite about some of the shadowy behaviors you may have taken note of earlier in this book when talking about behavior as a means of communication via the four functions.

Freewrite your thoughts about these shadowy behaviors here:

_____

_____

_____

_____

_____

_____

_____

Now explore these events using the ABC model and find common patterns in the situations or contexts in which they occur:

_____

_____

_____

_____

_____

_____

_____

_____

_____

_____

_____

_____

⚡ Integration Tip

Using this model (and other aspects of your knowledge about the shadow) can also shift how you relate to others. When you realize your own shadows, you make it easier to communicate your needs clearly to others, which helps you be authentic and integrate aspects of yourself that you may have previously stuffed down in your social interactions or close relationships. A side benefit is that you will understand the behavior of others better as well, and particularly with the ABC model you may be able to thwart tricky situations in the future.

Understanding that all behavior is functional and communicative in some way brings earthshaking shifts in your consciousness. Look, the unconscious is unconscious, which means you are not ever going to know why you do 100 percent of the things you do 100 percent of the time. However, by training your understanding to conscientiously view behavior in this way, you not only gain valuable understanding of yourself, but of other people as well. Earlier in this book you explored how a side effect of shadow work is less projection and judgment of others. This topic right here is a crystal fucking clear example of that. When you allow yourself to understand that all behavior, from giving a hug to acting like a world-class asshole, is somehow serving some unseen purpose/function, you begin to extend grace to both yourself and those outside of you. You begin to understand that truly, everyone is a flawed human being having a flawed human experience, and acting accordingly.

Chapter 25

Be Your Own Guide
Crafting Your Shadow Care Plan

So far in this workbook we have covered a number of things that are essential to not only conceptualizing the shadow, but also helping you create tools to face and integrate these shadows. These include:

- Understanding triggers and core wounds

- Learning about the functions of the shadow

- Identifying how we feel our shadows in our bodies

- Understanding the subconscious beliefs and programs we are working with

- Looking at how we've interpreted ourselves and our lives thus far

The more personal understanding you can gain when it comes to your shadows, the better. You will always be best served to become an expert on your own inner world in order to move forward.

This workbook has gone over a variety of topics intended to help you sort out some of these pieces, so you can put them all together in an integrative way that is totally personal to you and your shadows. For example, the fill-in-the-blanks part of Chapter 15 is a process you can use again and again to unfuck your responses to being triggered. So is the ABC model.

And as you get deeper into the different aspects of your shadows and begin untangling the patterns and behaviors surrounding them, you can also start crafting your own unique care plans based on all this knowledge and practice.

Fill It Out

Fill out the following as many times as needed. Ideally, this is an ongoing process you can turn to when moving forward with your shadow work, even once you have completed this workbook. This process of inquiry is to find focus points on where to turn your healing efforts for lasting integration.

Fill in the blanks to explore focus points for your healing efforts:

Situation that triggered me:

_____

_____

_____

The core wound it triggered: _____

How it made me feel, behave, or respond:

_____

_____

_____

_____

Did this response serve a purpose?

      ○ Yes   ○ No

If yes, what need was it meeting or function was it serving?

_____

_____

_____

How can I get that need met in a different way where I am consciously addressing the situation?

_____

_____

_____

_____

Thinking long-term solutions, is there something I can work on to neutralize the trigger?

_____

_____

_____

_____

Now, as counterintuitive as it may seem, this workbook also discussed the importance of *not* doing the work sometimes. This is big "know when to hold 'em, know when to fold 'em" energy! Sometimes shadow work can be exhausting. Sometimes it can be painful. Sometimes it can be easier to just think *fuck it!* and throw your hands up and let the shadowy forces within you be left alone to do their thing.

The reality is that those are all very good options sometimes. Only *you* will know which is the appropriate and best response at any given time.

In Chapter 21, you learned about how facing the shadow isn't all sunshine and rainbows. If you need a refresher, feel free to return to that chapter. Essentially, the point was this: Everything has its time and space, and not every time and space is the *right* time.

Use the following tips to help you navigate through the times when shadow work is simply not hitting the spot or going well:

- **Take breaks.** It's important to be strong and disciplined when embarking on any healing work, but it's also important to trust when you just don't have the mental, emotional, and energetic resources available. If you're feeling some resistance to shadow work or your integration efforts, you might just need to tap out for a bit. This is totally okay. Just like you wouldn't force yourself to roller-skate on two broken legs, you shouldn't force yourself to do shadow work when you're not emotionally or mentally strong enough to not have it be an absolutely dog shit experience.

- **Seek help.** Although this has been touched on earlier, it bears repeating: Some shadows have deep roots in trauma and engaging in this work can be triggering and counterproductive when it comes to healing. If you have access to professional help to aid in navigating these choppy waters, don't hesitate to use it. This is part of self-trust (knowing what you need to thrive and allowing yourself to have it). There are a variety of coaches, therapists, counselors, shamans, or other spiritual workers that can help guide you on this work. Trust yourself and recognize you do not need to do this shit alone.

- **Embrace imperfection.** Part of surrendering to the human experience is embracing imperfection. Perfection is not necessary, required, or even possible. Your most perfect state is a state of imperfection. This is what is natural for you. Anything else is bullshit escapist fantasy.

- **Be okay with not knowing.** Sometimes you may embark on a shadow work process and won't be able to figure it out. Sometimes you may be left perplexed, annoyed, and feeling more behind than when you started. The unconscious is always going to be mysterious and difficult to access and understand. This is why even dreams and symbols have a powerful place in the shadow work conversation. Sometimes you just gotta surrender to not knowing and not having the convenience of answers. Wanting to control and have it all figured out is a shadow too, after all.

- **Follow the natural timing of it all.** Just as you cannot fight repression with repression, you cannot force yourself into doing the work. When shadow work is doing more harm than good, just put it down. If you're in a space of needing a wee wallow, honor that shit. Timing is everything, and it's not always the right time.

Ultimately when it comes to creating a care plan for shadow work, you also need a care plan for *not* doing the work.

Write It Out

The following prompts are meant to help you gain an understanding of when it might be a good time to press pause on your shadow work efforts. You know yourself best, so it is important to set yourself up for success by honoring your mental and emotional limits when necessary.

Read the following prompts and reflect:

I will know when it is not the time to actively pursue shadow work when:

_____

_____

_____

I recognize that not actively doing the work at any given point is different than giving up entirely because:

_____

_____

_____

When things get too challenging I will do the following:

_____

_____

_____

When I need to wallow in my feelings I will do so in the following way(s):

_____

_____

_____

When I need to have boundaries with the wallowing I will do the following to move past it:

_____

_____

_____

Here are three affirming and loving statements I can repeat to myself when I am experiencing frustration with the shadow work process:

1. _____

2. _____

3. _____

Since shadow work is an ongoing process throughout the lifespan, make sure to revisit these prompts as often as you need to when a little extra self-care is in order.

Chapter 26

Filling the Void
Vision Boarding Your Post-Integration Self

It is typical human nature to compulsively want to fill a void. This is why we stuff those void spaces of the things we don't understand with our own assumptions and projections, and why we keenly feel the judgments from others who don't understand us. This is something that once you see, you cannot *unsee*, and it can help you take absolutely nothing personally, and learn to view things outside of yourself with a lot fewer assumptions.

When you illuminate your shadows and start to unfuck your programmed beliefs, etc., it creates a situation where you would be wise to intentionally fill in any blanks you may be leaving.

Throughout this book you've explored the ways that the shadow operates in your subconscious to influence your conscious understanding and experience. Just to make it *crystal* clear again: This is a totally normal part of the human experience. However, if you want to take your power back *after* illuminating the shadows and the complex ways they pop up in your life, you need to bring intention into the equation.

"Intention" is basically having a plan or target for something you're working toward. To live intentionally means you have clear aims in sight for the way you want to be, feel, and live, and that those intentions are what guide the shit you do and do not do.

Write It Out

Explore what living with intention would look like:

1. What would living intentionally look and feel like for you?

_____

_____

_____

_____

_____

2. Do you have a clear idea of what your intentions are and why?

_____

_____

_____

_____

_____

3. Do you have an idea of what shadowy interference may be standing in the way?

_____

_____

_____

_____

_____

Because we are all flawed human beings having a flawed human experience, we often operate in the space between living intentionally and living out the bullshit from our subconscious. Getting yanked back and forth between these forces can feel like we're pawns of quarreling parents on the verge of divorce. Again, this is totally normal, and if you can approach this work in the spirit of levity and acceptance, finding it funny even, you can bring the spirit of play and curiosity into your healing efforts!

You can rail against it all you want or you can recognize what a truly hilarious and confusing conundrum it is to be a conscious animal with creative reason and intelligence. It's truly up to you.

Life's a circus, baby!

Although everyone lives with some level of intention, the more you can approach life as an empowered cocreator (whether on the topic of shadow work or beyond), the better results you are going to get. In the previous chapters you've delved into some shadowy fuckery that may actually be interfering with your ability to gain clarity when it comes to crafting a vision for your intentional life, including:

- Zoning out and living on autopilot.
- Carrying programmed beliefs or shit worldviews that are unsupportive and make life feel out of control.
- Having shadows of perpetual victimhood or learned helplessness that somehow absolve you of responsibility in insidious ways.
- Believing deep down you aren't worthy of your desires.
- And more.

In the next sections, let's get real with how shadows have been messing with your ability to lead an intentional life.

Fill It Out

Fill out the following prompts for one specific shadowy issue you've uncovered while working through this book.
Feel free to use this prompt structure for other shadows in a separate notebook or journal.

Through the process of this workbook, I have discovered a few ways that my shadows have been impacting my life.

One of the things I've discovered that I would like to address first is:

_____

_____

This issue is worth addressing first because it impacts my life by:

_____

_____

_____

A more supportive vision for my life when this shadow is integrated would be:

_____

_____

_____

Because shadow work is a life's work (*sorry, not sorry*), it's important to note that there will always be barriers to clarity, and the tension will always exist between operating from the subconscious and living in an intentional way. This is simply an uncomfortable fact, like death or taxes. However, this doesn't mean that it's hopeless or not worth working through. It just means that your quest for clarity will always be a fulfilling source of learning for you.

Life does not come with a road map or a guidebook. Although this sounds like a nihilist take, it's actually kind of a thrill. The exciting thing about it is that you get to form your own map, and tap into your own guidance within yourself. You are truly the only one who even has a shred of a chance at influencing the direction you are moving in in real time. You are the only one who gets to be intimate with the inner workings of your conscious awareness at any given moment. And when you craft a vision with clarity, you are creating your *own* road map that you can consult, revamp, and clear barriers to, any time you choose.

So have fun with it. Just make sure you give yourself the chance to work this out and explore your vision so you aren't just left with voids waiting to be filled. This gets to be your compass and your motivation. It gets to be your hope and your empowerment. It gets to be a constantly evolving work in progress (much like you yourself are!). What it *isn't* is an ideal to measure yourself up to—something to feel like you are falling short of.

Vision It Out

Throughout the process of doing this book, you've likely discovered a few things about the way your shadows have been tainting the hidden corners of your life. It's time to craft a vision of what you would like your life to look and feel like in contrast—a road map for healing, but also motivation for pushing through the inner work, even when it gets hard.

Brainstorm your thoughts on the following questions:

1. What would you like to see in your life?

_____

_____

_____

_____

2. How would you like to feel?

_____

_____

_____

_____

3. What motivates you?

_____

_____

_____

_____

Now use what you've written to create a vision board.
You can use cut-out or printed-out images and/or words on an actual poster board, or digitally. If you are doing this digitally, Canva is a free and simple-to-use app with tons of images; you can also upload your own images and insert your own text.

⟨ Integration Tip
We need to tread lightly when talking about intention-setting and crafting more supportive visions for ourselves in the context of shadow work. Although this is a necessary part of empowering ourselves post-integration, this can sometimes circle back to that toxic issue of treating yourself as if you are a problem that needs to be fixed. If this perspective is creeping up for you, cut that shit out with love by reminding yourself that this is not an intentional perspective that is rooted in truth. You are not a problem that needs fixing; you are a constantly evolving work of art that deserves the very best life experience available on a rolling, ongoing basis.

Chapter 27

Let It Go
Releasing Resistance to Integration

Earlier in this workbook we touched on resistance, and how the ego struggles to get out of the way when we're facing our shadows head-on. Resistance, or the ego-driven desire to make difficult feelings, hard truths, or the inconvenience of "doing the work" just go away, is part of the shadow work process throughout. When it comes to integration, resistance can ramp up in intensity. The reason for this is that integrating your shadows is a direct challenge to your ego. It's a conscious acknowledgment of parts of you that the ego has directly repressed somewhere along the way.

It's important to revisit and dig deeper into the concept of resistance when it comes to integration of the shadow, as it can and will pop up in any and all parts of shadow work, contributing to the ongoing nature of the work.

The kind of resistance you can face is often tied to the level of "unacceptability" you perceive in any given shadow. You may face less resistance when acknowledging the hidden gems of your personality, and more when recognizing all the sneaky ways you might be the direct perpetrator of the bullshit in your life.

Personal responsibility is one of the most important aspects of facing the shadow. Because the reality is that some of the biggest shadows are hidden in plain sight, and are the most repellent for the ego. It can be hard to recognize when you may be the one participating in your own "stuckness" and lack of healing. Take a look at the following examples that contribute to this feeling of "stuckness," and check in with your body to see if you have a resistance response to any of these statements:

- Maintaining a victim persona can be a form of manipulation.

- Resistance to addressing insecurity can be a way for you to gain validation from others.

- Allowing anger to control your life can allow you to feel in control and absolve you of taking responsibility for your emotions.

In many cases, the shadows we resist facing and integrating the most are the ones that serve the function of absolving us from responsibility in some way. There is an undeniable yet complex relationship between martyrdom, helplessness, and the shadow. The shadow is a master at keeping us in positions of feeling disempowered and reaping all the surface-level comforts of not having to take responsibility or risks for our growth.

Feel It Out

Reflect on the following related to the examples of "stuckness":

1. How did you feel reading these examples?

_____

_____

_____

_____

_____

_____

2. Can you think of some additional examples of hard shadowy truths that cause resistance for you, and why?

_____

_____

_____

_____

_____

_____

3. Explore the emotions that come up as you reflect, then write down what you experienced:

_____

_____

_____

_____

_____

_____

It was discussed in an earlier chapter, but deserves repeating: The cold hard fact is that if doing shadow work *only* leaves you feeling vindicated, triumphant, comfortable, or excited, then you probably need to dig a little deeper. This isn't to say you must necessarily suffer to work with the shadow, but the real juicy bits come when you humble yourself to experience a gut punch in the feels, or recognize within yourself the flare of resistance.

It might sound repetitive, but this shit is worth being reminded of again and again during this journey: One of the most challenging elements of shadow work is both honoring the circumstances in your past that may have left you in a space of victimhood or trauma, and taking responsibility to avoid treading so lightly around your wounds that you marinade in a space of disempowerment for too long. This takes a focused commitment to being open and nonjudgmental when approaching your shadows, and working on your self-trust and empowerment.

All healing has to strike a balance between being kind and gentle with yourself, and picking yourself up out of the mud and giving yourself a loving kick in the ass. There truly is no sugarcoating it.

Although the topic of resistance was explored previously, it deserves additional emphasis because it is by far one of the most sneaky and challenging blocks to integration. Shadow work is only going to do you good when you can plow through the resistance to your personal responsibility in your life, rather than letting your ego go back to business as usual (repressing the things that you can't bear to face).

Behaviors or patterns that indicate a resistance to integrating your shadows are things like:

- Expecting others to tiptoe around your triggers.
- Identifying too closely with a victimhood narrative.
- Consistently blaming others for your circumstances or feelings.
- Being angry at other people for not doing the things you would like or fulfilling your needs.
- Carrying binary ideas of being "right" or "wrong" without acknowledging other perspectives.
- Feeling as if you are owed something and postponing happiness until this debt is paid.
- Carrying stories that make your progress contingent on the participation of others.

Write It Out

If you want to face resistance head-on so you can release it and move forward, allow yourself to be brutally honest and explore your reactions and responses to the following prompts.

Reflect on the following questions, and be as honest as possible:

1. Is there a part of you that feels comfortable in victimhood?

_____

_____

_____

_____

2. Is there a part of you that craves control?

_____

_____

_____

_____

3. Is there a part of you that's addicted to drama?

_____

_____

_____

_____

4. Where are you participating in your own struggle?

_____

_____

_____

_____

5. How is lingering in your shadows potentially benefiting you?

_____

_____

_____

_____

Inside you are two gremlins. One is ultimately sick of the bullshit and full of longing for something better, and one wears all the wounds, martyrdom, and helplessness like a warm, weighted blanket. The secret is that they both deserve your attention and your ear, and they both need to be honored, loved, and integrated. Your goal is not to get rid of either of them, or to prefer one over the other. Your goal is not to give either of them any sort of differential value in terms of "goodness" or "badness." They both have their place and their purpose, and truly only you will know when it's appropriate to lead your actions with each!

You are both of these gremlins, and both of them are you.

Ultimately, resistance is an unavoidable part of the process. However, it doesn't need to limit your growth or forward motion if you approach the presence of it as an invitation to go a little deeper, and to get a little more honest. You can approach this gently—but it should also be approached with strength.

Chapter 28

Don't Get Stuck
Trusting Yourself and Your Shadow

In Phase 1 of shadow work, it's very normal to feel a lot of resentment or resistance to the ways the shadow manifests itself in your life. In the perception phase, it becomes clear just how entangled the shadow influence is in your daily experience, relationships, and self-concept, and this can be jarring to say the least!

However, as we move forward through the investigation phase and into the integration phase, a clearer picture begins to come into focus: Your shadow is often a misunderstood teacher—and understanding it as such can unlock self-trust.

As you make mistakes and act in ways you aren't always proud of, it's easy to beat yourself up, which can lead to negative feelings that impact how competent and confident you feel. However, the reality is that your ego and your shadow selves are all on your team…just perhaps not on the same page yet! If you can reconceptualize even your biggest mistakes as sneaky attempts toward trying to feel safe and whole, you can begin building trust in your choices, your ability to discern what is important, what you are capable of, and a whole lot more.

Sometimes shadow work happens in a journal, and sometimes it happens in taking scary leaps of action. But all encounters with the shadow should be appreciated as doorways into new levels of understanding that will ultimately serve to benefit *you*.

Write It Out

Write a letter of gratitude to your shadows as a way to reframe your "missteps" in the spirit of understanding their potentially protective purpose. Whether it be to a specific shadow that you've identified, or your whole shadow team, try to approach understanding them through the lens of self-trust. Try to include specific elements of what function these shadows may be trying to serve, as explored in prior chapters. By this point in the work, you should be building a fuller picture of your shadows, including their motivations and origins.

In order to truly find integration, you must understand that the shadow is you and you are it. Your conscious mind has no right to judge the things that have been unconscious, and you must accept yourself in the wholeness of who you are—shadowy bits and all! This will require trusting what it is trying to teach you.

Your shadow is as much a part of you as your curiosity, your creativity, or your ability to love. Do not get stuck in a trap of wishing for "shadow healing" in the sense of fixing anything. You have to trust in yourself and in your shadow, that these are all elements of the complex and brilliant whole of who you are. This is not work that has a finish line, standards to live up to, or rules in terms of "right" versus "wrong" ways to do it. This is relationship building, which means it will always be a complex dynamic process. If you set a goalpost, recognize its gonna move. Just like any relationship with a partner or friend, you never hit a point where you are finished getting to know them or nurturing the relationship. This isn't a bad thing either—it's actually exciting, expansive, and full of novelty!

In many cases, shadow integration is about humbling yourself enough to recognize that you are simply a human being having a human experience, and there are conscious and unconscious elements of that. The real sauce comes from accepting and even embracing the shit out of this!

Write your shadow a letter of gratiude, be specific about how this shadow has served you and made you who you are today:

Dear _____ ,

_____

_____

_____

_____

_____

_____

_____

_____

_____

_____

_____

_____

_____

_____

_____

_____

_____

_____

_____

Love, _____

Sign It Out

Read and initial each statement, customizing as necessary, making a promise and commitment to honoring this work even when it feels messy and imperfect:

_____ I understand that I am an imperfect human being having an imperfect human experience.

_____ I understand that my shadow side is an imperfect dimension of the imperfect human that I am.

_____ I trust that an encounter with my shadow is really just an opportunity to learn, and I trust it.

_____ I do not require the process, the results, or any part of this to be perfect.

_____

[Sign Here]

You do not need to be some high-level ascended master or some profoundly enlightened being to integrate your shadows. You just need to be willing to be imperfect and willing to engage yourself with curiosity and compassion. You know you are capable of doing this because you easily extend this energy to others. It doesn't have to be a heavy thing or major challenge. It just…_is_!

Self-trust is the best tool you can have available in your healing arsenal. This will help you know when it's time to do the work, and when it's time to take a break. It will let you trust in your decisions, and it will let you be okay with being flawed. A part of self-trust is also trusting the unique and powerful role of the shadow. This is not a foe to be vanquished; it is a hidden treasure to be found. Even though the shadow may communicate with you in ways you do not appreciate or understand, it _is_, at its core, a communication of sorts. It's only when you accept this that you will allow yourself to be authentically free.

So see every trigger as an invitation, every shadowy encounter as an enticement to woo the parts of you that have been hidden and cut off for far too long. Your life and your connection to yourself will need to include an ongoing courtship of your shadow.

Trust that this is a very good and useful thing, despite how often it may shock and inconvenience you!

Integration Tip

Part of the reason for approaching the shadow in the spirit of levity and play is to make it something that is tinged with excitement and curiosity rather than a chore that feels too big and monstrous for you to handle. Trust yourself and trust your shadow. Trust that you are not a problem to be fixed; you are a brilliantly complex creature to be appreciated. As much as you can, take the very human judgments out of the equation and just let things be what they are, and appreciate the many authentic sides of you.

Chapter 29

Control Freak
Letting Go of Martyrdom, Perfection, and Victimhood

Of all the shadows that have an absolute choke hold on our lives, one of the strongest is that of the martyr or perpetual victim. In fact, I would argue that this shadow in particular is one of *the* most important to face if you want to truly shift your experience of life in hyperspeed. While you have read a bit about this shadow earlier in this workbook, this chapter provides a deeper look, along with guidance in integrating it into your authentic self and life.

⚡ Integration Tip
There is no time limit on shadow work. It is definitely the work of the ego to want to speed things up, but the truth is that you can deliberately choose to face hard things and reduce the amount of time you spend letting the unconscious fuck with your peace. You can work smarter not harder, not by rushing yourself, but by recognizing whether you are treading too lightly to avoid facing some of your more difficult shadows.

The martyr or career victim shadow (you may know this one as the "martyr complex" in psychology) is when someone participates in or perpetuates their own suffering, which usually fills shadowy needs of obtaining attention, resources, or avoiding personal responsibility.

It also coexists with the concept of being singled out or persecuted for being "different" or "special" in some way.

This shadow is sometimes paired with having issues of codependency and wobbly boundaries. Codependency is a tendency in imbalanced relationships where you may sacrifice your own peace or independence to please the other person (who may then encourage you to remain in a "helpless" state). Wobbly boundaries are those instances where you allow others to ignore the things you have determined to be your comfortable limits, or you are inconsistent with ensuring your own safety and independence in relationships.

The thing about the career victim shadow is that you can likely identify people in your life who fit the profile. However, it can be difficult to face it within yourself, and for good reason: Do you think the ego is just gonna be chill about recognizing that maybe you're being a lil' manipulative and suffering needlessly? Hell no.

Now, sometimes even just a hint of this can challenge the ego into being triggered in a big way. This is a *good* and normal thing. But let's remember some basic hard truths about shadow healing that can set you free:

- Every trigger is an invitation.
- Nobody else is responsible for your healing and growth.
- Sometimes you are your own worst enemy.

Draw It Out

Can you recognize whether you have a martyr shadow? Do you frequently feel like the victim in your relationships or life? Does the very idea of such a thing trigger the fuck out of you?

Sketch out a depiction of your martyr shadow here:

Earlier in this workbook, you learned a bit about perfectionism and how it may be cropping up among your shadows. It can also go deeper: Often, there is a strong correlation between martyrdom and ideals of perfection. This can manifest in setting impossible standards, both for yourself and for your relationships (the expectations that others can make you happy, or the desire to "score keep" factors in here). There can also be an element of justice-seeking, and clinging to righteousness and victimhood when you do not get the justice you're seeking or deserve.

I've said it before and I will say it again (with love!): Perfection doesn't exist. The only way to ensure you get healing is to go out there and mine for it yourself. Anytime you make your progress contingent on outside input, you are willingly giving away your power. You can waste your life rotting while waiting for closure that may never come.

In situations where you may have been the unwilling victim, scapegoated by others, or horrifically mistreated, the reality is that you are typically left holding the bag. In a perfect world, divine justice would rain down upon those who mistreated you, but the world is far from perfect and so are you. A lot of people carry unnecessary burdens as a badge of honor, sometimes for their entire lifetime. The cold hard truth about these badges is that they get absolutely no respect, recognition, or due.

The next prompt is meant to help you integrate the shadows of martyrdom and perfection, to help you get independence and strength separate from the idea that you need someone else to participate in your healing.

Fill It Out

Can you release a situation when you were left with an unpaid debt or lack of closure?

Use this prompt to guide you as you let things go on your own:

The situation I would like to release is:

_____

_____

_____

This situation left me in a place with the following emotional and practical consequences:

_____

_____

_____

The ending I desire is:

_____

_____

_____

The parts of this ending I have no control over are:

_____

_____

_____

The parts I do have some control over are:

_____

_____

_____

I can use this situation as a vehicle for growth by recognizing:

_____

_____

_____

I release the unpaid debt or desire for closure with love by:

_____

_____

_____

Victimhood and martyrdom may be serving your shadows and stalling you from moving forward. To be clear, this is *not* to say you should forgive and forget, or that the lasting issues you may have from trauma or truly dire circumstances are your fault. That is simply not the case. Just that at a certain point, shit happens—*dramatically unfair* shit—and it is your responsibility and duty to yourself to work through it and release what you can. Even if it's just from a space of spite (all routes to healing are valid!). In many cases, this could be the kind of intensive clearing you may need a therapist to help you through. It's all good! Ultimately, your life is limited in duration and it's absolutely not the best vibe to spend more years than necessary marinating in past shit that's already been and done.

The only reason why facing a victimhood shadow is difficult is because of the judgments associated with it. It's important to always remember that your shadows are *not* your conscious decisions. You cannot judge that which is unconscious! Coming back to the idea that shadows are misguided helpers, you can start releasing victimhood and martyrdom by recognizing them as such. Use the following prompt to thank them and look at them more lovingly.

Write It Out

Reflect on the following statements to reframe your shadows:

My martyr shadow is serving me in the following way:

_____

_____

_____

_____

Alternate ways I can serve those purposes or fulfill those needs might be:

_____

_____

_____

_____

Now, write a letter of gratitude to yourself, specifically your martyr shadow, thanking it for helping you fulfill your needs:

Dear _____,

_____

_____

_____

_____

_____

_____

_____

Love, _____

Write a letter of intention to your martyr shadow setting boundaries for how you want to work with it in the future in a way that is conscious and intentional:

Dear _____,

_____

_____

_____

_____

_____

_____

_____

Love, _____

Chapter 30

A Life's Work
Understanding Shadow Integration As a Lifelong Endeavor

Whenever I cover shadow work in my programs or courses I inevitably get the question: "When do you know when you're done doing the work?"

Well, if it's a finish line you're after, I have some bad news! The truth, as you've probably gleaned by now, is that the shadow is a part of you completely, so working with it is never a task that will reach completion. Whether we are aware of our shadow or not, whether we have done work with it or not, whether we are taking steps to integrate it or not, the shadow is a part of us. It is part of the complex whole of who we are, and it will always be present and have a seat at the chaotic banquet table of who we are.

The shadow is present whether you're meditating like a monk or cussing folks out in a rage-fueled breakdown on the street. The shadow just *is*. This is why courting it out of the subconscious into the conscious is so important and so foundational to your experience of life. The more aware of your shadow's influence you are, the more you are able to work with it. The more you understand and accept those maligned aspects of yourself, the more easily you can connect to your authenticity and live a life that's free of judgy bullshit.

This is about relationship building, *not* graduation.

Again, this is why you must do this work without judgment or self-flagellation. How likely would you be to get into a relationship with anybody who approached you with nothing but disdain and disgust? Seeing your shadowy bits as lovably imperfect parts of the whole of who you are, is part of the journey toward reclaiming your authenticity and transforming chaos into clarity.

⚡ Integration Tip

You know those movies where the villain becomes the bestie? Or the child and their boogeyman all of a sudden buddy up in a bizarrely heartwarming odd couple scenario? Conceptualize your ongoing relationship to your shadow as being something like that!

Sign It Out

It's time to make a recommitment to yourself and shadow work as an ongoing endeavor! Fill in the blanks and sign your name as an act of your continued commitment and total understanding that this shit is ongoing, important, and a gift you give yourself!

Read and initial each statement, customizing as necessary, making a promise and commitment to the ongoing process of shadow work:

_____ I, _____ , understand that shadow illumination and integration is a lifelong process, and I commit to giving myself the space and patience to recognize it as such.

_____ I commit to loving and accepting my integrated shadows as part of my "me-team."

If I catch myself getting caught up in the mind trap of feeling shitty that it's still not "over" and that I still have things to integrate, I will use the following affirmation to gently kick myself in the ass as a reminder that this is a lifelong journey of love and self-acceptance:

_____

_____

_____

_____

[Sign Here]

Just as you cannot fight repression with repression, you cannot get into a relationship with your shadows in the hopes that you can make them "go away." Just as you cannot make the sun's shadow leave (it only moves in relation to the parts illuminated), you cannot heal your shadow in a *curative* sense. The real magic of shadow healing and integration is less about chasing them off, and more about the dance of getting to know the ways they manifest in your life and awareness. It's about learning how to work with them rather than against them, and how to bring the medicine of self-discovery and curiosity to the wounds and pains they are associated with.

Ultimately, integration is the messy and humbling process of ceasing to externalize your shadow, and moving to a place of recognizing that you and your shadow are one and the same, and taking responsibility for that.

In Phases 1 and 2, you examined the shadow as an outside entity in order to get to know it better. Remember the example of fixing a computer? You may have to take out the motherboard or other parts in order to view it from all angles to get a closer look at what the issues are. However, you are not going to be able to make that computer fully functional again without putting all the pieces back together to make it whole. Now that you've reached the end of Phase 3, it's time to take all that information you've found and accept it back into the fold of who you are in your conscious awareness. Humbly. Acceptingly. And with a fuck-ton of love and compassion.

"Your shadow is triggered" is *you* being triggered.

"Your inner child needing some love" is *you* needing some love.

"Your shadowy wounds being triggered" is *you* getting an invitation to go deeper.

The more you begin to view the wholeness of yourself with compassion, forgiveness, and understanding, the more you will benefit from the privilege it is to get to know yourself in your authenticity on an ongoing basis.

Write It Out

Write a letter of acceptance to yourself, no longer externalizing your shadow in the language and descriptions you choose, but in the spirit of full acceptance that you and your shadow are one and the same. If you are not yet at a point where this feels comfortable (we are not trying to swerve into the lane of guilt, shame, or other resistance feelings), then revisit this at a later time.

You are your shadow. Your shadow is you. You are an ongoing work in progress. You are both the light and the dark. You are the freedom of authentic self-expression, and you are the one who looks on in judgment and fear. It is all you and you are all of it. It is glorious in its messy confusion and imperfect mechanics. You are truly a miracle of consciousness, free will, and curiosity. You are the work and the play and everything in between!

This is a gift and not a curse. This is the great work of alchemy. This is love, acceptance, and growth.

Dear _____ ,

_____

_____

_____

_____

_____

_____

_____

_____

_____

_____

_____

_____

_____

_____

_____

_____

_____

_____

_____

_____

_____

Love, _____

Talk It Out

Sit in front of an empty chair and imagine your shadow is sitting right there—your whole collection of shadowy characters uncovered earlier in this workbook. Move through these steps as a way of integrating those characters into your whole self (with conditions!). Let yourself fully feel into this activity.

Talk with your shadow:

1. State aloud that this is you and you are it.

2. Set boundaries with your shadow aloud, understanding that this is you setting boundaries with yourself. For example, being strict with your mindset when you begin beating yourself up, or taking responsibility for forming new habits that will actually serve where you're going rather than contributing to feelings of being "stuck."

3. Set the intention to commit to ongoing discovery and integration aloud.

4. Thank yourself aloud for taking responsibility for setting limits with your shadow.

5. Finally, write out what emotions came up for you.

_____

_____

_____

Conclusion
Illuminating the Path Forward

Now is the time to pause, take a deep breath, and celebrate yourself for embarking on this work. Pardon the cheesy, overused platitude, but the truth about personal development and healing work is that it truly is a marathon, not a sprint. There are folks who pick it up and drop it quickly after. There are folks who decide it's not for them. This is not a judgment since everyone is exactly where they choose to be depending on their level of readiness. It's just recognition that by reaching the end of this workbook, you've taken a huge leap toward unleashing your authenticity and transforming chaos to clarity! You are doing important work, and you deserve to be celebrated. Do not skip out on recognizing how important this is and giving yourself the credit that you're due!

As you move forward on your path through shadow work, feel free to pick this book up again and again, hop from chapter to chapter, and reengage with different activities within. As mentioned before, this is a lifelong process of inquiry. It doesn't need to be heavy. Think of what a privilege it is to essentially court yourself…getting to know deeper and deeper levels of the incredible creature you are. You are completely worthy of this act of self-love.

A Note on Healing Hangovers

Before moving forward, I wanted to cover a "footnote" kind of shadow you may encounter in the later stages of shadow work: a condition I call the dreaded "Healing Hangover"!

Healing can be a rush. Uncovering your shadowy subconscious programming and all the ways it may be manifesting in your life can be a thrilling and illuminating experience. A high like no other! Self-discovery can be fulfilling and addictive. But like any other high, it must be approached responsibly. It's important to have balance between doing the work and allowing yourself to integrate and just *be*.

Binge healing can often lead to healing hangovers. This is a state of burnout that can happen when you *work work work*, but don't take the opportunity to rest and just live. This can result in neglecting self-care, energetic burnout, overwhelm with the demon pile you've uncovered, frustration, and getting sucked into the spiral of perpetually seeking to find the next thing that needs fixing.

Exhausting.

The antidote is to take breaks and go live your life! Have pity-party days where you stay wrapped up in a blanket! This workbook is heavily focused on integration and repetitive about being nonjudgmental in healing because *you are not a problem to be solved.* You can both do the work to heal and deeply understand this fact at the same time. Reflect upon how far you've already come and rest in gratitude. Take the time to get into your life, play, laugh, fuck things up, smile, and bask in your humanness!

A Final Pep Talk

The end of any workbook, course, program, or other guided personal development offering can be bittersweet. There can be a sense of both triumph and apprehension about heading forward into the unknown. My intention with the format and content of this book was to give you the confidence and tools to engage with your shadow in an ongoing way as you move through life. As stated before, this is a lifelong process of inquiry, discovery, and integration—one that gets to be fun, empowering, and healing!

Please remember that you don't need to be perfect. You don't need to make your shadow "go away." You don't need to be limited by old wounds and programming in perpetuity. Move forward in your path in the spirit of curiosity, play, and radical self-acceptance. Move forward in the spirit of gratitude for yourself, and with the knowledge that you have the power to hack your life experience to feel more authentic and free. See every trigger as an invitation, and every surprise encounter with your shadow as a chance to understand yourself more deeply.

Embrace your authenticity with the respect and reverence it deserves! May your life be filled with the kind of love and light that both you *and* your shadows have always craved and been deeply and infinitely worthy of.

About the Author

Mandi Em is a humorist, author, and chaotic wellness witch. She's the author of *Witchcraft Therapy*, *Feral Self-Care,* and *Happy Witch*, and she shares funny, approachable self-help guidance on her blog and social channels at *Healing for Hot Messes*, along with resources for nonreligious witches over at *The Secular Witch*. Her writing has been featured in *The New York Times*, *HuffPost*, *SheKnows*, *Refinery29*, *McSweeney's*, and more. She and her husband are born-again hippies raising their three children in beautiful Vernon, British Columbia, in Canada.